Financially Free

About the author

Anne Hartley began her career in her late 20's as a single mother of two living on $45.00 a week. She set up a typing business at home and has never looked back. She now owns a financial planning company called Prosperity Network.

In her work as a financial planner and in her successful 'Financially Free' courses, Anne encourages women to set their goals and change their attitudes to money before they make any investment choices. She emphasises the importance of enjoying money in the present as well as planning for the future.

Over the years, Anne has contributed to *Cleo, Womens Weekly* and *Rydges*. She now lives in Sydney with her two daughters. In her spare time she enjoys reading and gardening.

Financially Free

THINK RICH TO BE RICH

A woman's guide to creating wealth

ANNE HARTLEY

DOUBLEDAY
SYDNEY   AUCKLAND   NEW YORK   TORONTO   LONDON

To Lisa, Robert and Laura.
What a difference you made in my life.

FINANCIALLY FREE

First published in Australasia in 1990 by Doubleday,
a division of Transworld Publishers (Aust.) Pty Limited
15–25 Helles Avenue, Moorebank NSW 2170

National Library of Australia
Cataloguing-in-Publication data

Hartley, Anne, 1946–
    Financially Free: a woman's guide to creating wealth.
    Bibliography.
    Includes index.
    ISBN 0 86824 3892

    1. Women—Finance, Personal. 2. Women—Attitudes.
    3. Women in business. I. Title.

332.02042

Cover design by Trevor Hood
Typeset in Australia by Midland Typesetters
Printed in Australia by The Book Printer

Contents

Acknowledgements

I'd like to thank my daughter Lisa for her loving support and encouragement and her help in typing the manuscript. Thanks to my friends Jenny, Les and Ian, for their valued contributions.

A special thanks to Doubleday for making this task so easy, and I'm especially grateful to my clients, and all the people who have attended a 'Financially Free' course.

Most of all thanks to my Mum, who always told me that I could do anything.

Preface
How it all began

I first became interested in prosperity because I had no money.

During the mid-seventies I was living as a single parent with my two children, finding it difficult to exist on a government pension. As I searched for a way out, I discovered that my thoughts created my world. I realised that I did not have to be a victim of circumstances. If I, alone, controlled my life, then I could change it.

I had always been interested in positive thinking, but it only worked for a time, with opportunities coming and going just as quickly, and I kept returning to my original state of just scraping by. As with many other people, my problems arose from my beliefs about money of which I was unaware. Only when I began to work on discovering and changing my deep-seated preconceptions did I experience lasting success.

At the time of my first business venture, I was living in a very dilapidated half-house, which was all I could afford. My neighbours fought day and night. Cockroaches lay in wait for me, despite all efforts with pesticides and cleanliness. My son was just a baby and I did not want to leave him, to return to full-time work. The whole situation was definitely outside my comfort zone. A business that I could run from home and a better home, seemed the logical solution.

Weighing up the pros and cons, I had typing and bookkeeping skills on the positive side. On the other hand, I had no experience in sales or promotion, no potential clients, no typewriter or equipment, no area to set aside for a work space, and no money. Just the same, I wasn't going to stay where I was, so my motivation was high.

Firstly, I told everyone I knew that I was operating a typing and bookkeeping service. Within two days a workmate of a friend rang, wanting a thesis typed. I had never typed a thesis, but undeterred said I'd be happy to do it. When he asked what kind of typewriter I had, I automatically responded 'an IBM'. He told me the standard rate and after hiring an IBM (on borrowed money), working from a kitchen table, my business was under way.

Gaining confidence, I decided to promote my service to the many small businesses operating in the surrounding districts. I then met a man at a party who taught printing. I told him what I wanted to do. He set his students the assignment of designing, typesetting and printing promotional brochures. All at no cost to me. The quality of work was first class. Within six months I had sufficient income to move to a much better house and was back to where I felt comfortable.

What happened? Nothing mysterious. My desire for a better home far outweighed the negatives that surrounded me. I set a goal, broke it down into small pieces and focused on what I wanted, rather than how to achieve it.

That was where my search for prosperity began. Since then I have started two other businesses and sold both at a profit, but it hasn't always been smooth sailing. I had a lot of negative programs about money that have taken years to clear. Like many other people I went through a period of not knowing what I wanted to do. In my mid-thirties I had a complete mid-life crisis, and felt unsure about where I was going, and what I wanted to do with the rest of my life.

I applied the same methods to solve this dilemma that

I applied to starting my first business. Although I didn't know what I wanted to do, I still had an overall image of the life that I wanted to live, so I broke my goals into small pieces, and made a list of the things that I enjoyed doing. As difficult as it was I tried to keep my focus on the life I wanted to lead rather than the confusion that surrounded me, and eventually when the perfect job finally did come along, I was able to recognise it. How I attracted this job to me is explained more fully in a later chapter.

They say we teach best what we most need to learn, and money had always been a major issue in my life, so it was natural that I should gravitate towards a career as a financial planner. I now have a very diverse group of private clients. Private clients in this instance mean individuals, rather than corporations. I advise on everything from joining a superannuation scheme and investing, through to retirement planning. Some clients have no money, or unmanageable debts, others need advice on how to invest varying sums of money, sometimes amounting to millions. At first it seemed strange that I, who had so many financial problems, should advise others on how to manage theirs, but my experiences have given me a greater depth of knowledge of all financial situations, and more understanding.

After I began this work, I realised that all the practical advice in the world will make no difference if the whole person is not treated. If we do not change our belief system, then we will keep returning to a level at which we feel comfortable, even if this is a state of deprivation. So the idea for this book and a course where I could explain the laws of prosperity in more depth than I could at a personal consultation was born. This course, also called 'Financially Free' is based on my own experiences and the methods I used to change my life, combined with some practical financial skills. The course has been running for three years now and people from all walks of life from doctors to students have attended.

Many others beside myself have practised the principles as outlined in this book, and they have worked. There have been times for me when nothing worked, and I would wonder what I was doing wrong. But I am persistent and I discovered that commitment to applying the principles, even when nothing appears to be going right, is what makes the difference.

The course has grown as well, and will soon be available all over Australia. I believe that only by shifting mass consciousness to prosperity, will our nation's economic problems be solved.

I hope you will join me in being financially free. The methods work . . . if you do.

Introduction

What does FINANCIAL FREEDOM mean to you? To one person it could be having millions of dollars. To another it might simply be holding down a job. Ten different people would have ten different answers.

Self-esteem seems to be linked to money. We judge our success or failure by the size of our pay packet, or the quality of our possessions. Money can represent status, security, or a sign to the world of how smart we are. It can be a constant source of worry, or it can give immense pleasure. But why are some people successful with money and others not?

Many people believe that there is no way they can become wealthy. Yet, the average worker on an ordinary salary will earn in excess of a million dollars over a thirty year working life. If this same worker saved just 10 per cent of her income and invested it at 10 per cent, she would accumulate over $500 000. An astute investor can do much better than this, and not only wealthy people can have investments.

So how do we come by our beliefs? Mostly through childhood conditioning. We all have ingrained beliefs in our subconscious, about a whole range of subjects. In some families money is a dirty word. You can talk about politics, sex, or religion, but NEVER tell anyone how much money you have, or don't have. For some people the mere mention of the word *money* can cause instant depression.

Nationality plays a large part. For instance, the English

tend to be very conservative and loathe to discuss financial matters even with other family members. In direct contrast, Greeks or Italians tend to be more open, sometimes including their children in financial consultations. Many Chinese are conditioned to believe you have to work hard to make money.

Our western society has been conditioned to believe that we can only succeed by living on credit, often beyond our means. We have become a credit card generation, and expectations of today's generation are different to those of our parents, who would often save for years rather than borrow money. This trend has encouraged many people to live beyond their means and the statistics support that this trend is growing. In 1987, 70 per cent of all bankrupts were under twenty-five, mainly because of overspending on credit. This credit is usually not used to build assets, but to purchase goods that are easily disposable such as cars, clothes, records, compact disc players. Credit is often used to support lifestyles well beyond peoples' means, and bills, food, even holidays are charged so that payment is deferred to some future date. We cannot allow this trend to continue.

Women who make money through their own resources are still a minority group. Most women with substantial sums have either inherited it; come into money from a divorce settlement; or their husbands have earned it. Such women can be fearful of losing what they have because they mistakenly believe that they only have one chance that will not come again. Such fearfulness can cost them money, because they leave money in bank accounts earning low interest rates, in the belief that only banks have safe investments. Too many people have never been encouraged to learn even the basics about money management.

This book is not just for people with a shortage of money. Money can be a source of worry for some who have immense wealth. It is not the amount of money that you have that is important, it is how you feel about it. Having advised hundreds of people on money matters, I've discovered that there is little point in giving practical financial advice to people who are impoverished in their thinking. Our beliefs will either sabotage us, or help us to succeed. Which would you prefer? When you shift your focus off your money problems and onto your goals, then you have begun the process of developing a prosperity consciousness.

This book is about people, ordinary people, who have overcome obstacles to achieve their dreams. There are no get-rich-quick schemes, but there are many success stories. Your dreams are important. You may aim to become a millionaire, want to be paid to work at a hobby, or, you may not yet be sure of what you want. This book is about self-discovery, about being comfortable with who you are, and what you have, right now.

I cannot guarantee to change your life. Only you can do that. I can guarantee that the principles outlined in this book do work.

PART ONE

Changing your Attitudes

CHAPTER 1

Prosperity: choice not chance

Prosperity means different things to different people. To me it means more than just money—it means total abundance in all areas of my life; my work, family, relationships and lifestyle. Money is merely a commodity that allows me to enjoy these things more.

A great number of motivational books seem to be written for people who want to get rich and that's fine, but not everyone wants to be rich. Many want to be able to achieve their goals and live a life free of money worries. Whatever your goal, it is achievable because there is no such thing as luck. We create our world by the choices we make. Some of us are more fortunate in circumstances of birth and education, but ultimately what we make of our lives and our finances is up to us.

Money problems affect people from all socio-economic groups. Among my clients are wealthy widows, for whom money represents security and who are so fearful of making the wrong decision that they don't make any at all. There are outwardly successful career women who overspend on credit cards, often to compensate for a lack in other areas of their lives. There are men burdened by the responsibility of being the sole providers, reluctant to admit to their lack of knowledge. Others simply do not earn enough to live. At one time I was one of the latter group and it was only when I began to work on discovering my deep-seated preconceptions about money that I experienced lasting success, in overcoming my financial difficulties.

What makes you feel prosperous?

Changing your thoughts is the most important thing you can do. But if you really want to attain wealth, you also need some practical knowledge.We live in times of change, and laws relating to taxation, investments and our entire financial structure are in a constant state of flux. Fortunately, no-one needs to have a degree in economics or to be a whiz at maths to make money. No-one ever became wealthy on a wage. You must invest money in order to multiply it. You could make an investment in bonds, shares, property, or you could invest in a business of your own. Your options are only limited by your imagination. Investments do not have to be boring or hard work and making money can be fun. The acquisition of a holiday home or work of art might be overlooked as an enjoyable form of investment, yet such purchases have great potential for increasing in value.

There are no hopeless cases and there is no virtue in poverty. Anyone can prosper by taking charge of their thoughts, and asking for help if necessary. You can start by deciding what makes you feel prosperous.

One of my clients, Frances, found that her financial situation improved when she decided to include luxury items in her basic budget.

When Frances first came to see me, she thought she was a hopeless case. Like many people with money problems, she was on the defensive. 'Coming here today is the hardest thing I've ever done. It's like admitting I'm a failure, and there's probably nothing you can do anyway.'

Frances's story

Frances is a librarian, divorced and earning a good income. She had a problem with credit cards. Her debts included a personal loan, loans from two family members and seven credit card accounts. The monthly repayments were crippling her, and she was being hounded by creditors.

At first we worked on a purely practical level. We arranged a consolidation loan to clear all debts and then organised a budget so she could cover all expenses.

In the following months I saw Frances periodically. Sometimes she made progress; sometimes she slipped back into her old ways. We experimented with different methods of budgeting until we found one that worked. At one time, after running up her credit cards again, Frances decided to withdraw the last bit of money that she had invested with a finance company. At that time she was particularly stressed, as this meant she would have no money to fall back on. The money was invested for a long term, and although Frances was withdrawing early, the man from the finance company went out of his way to help her, without having any knowledge of her situation. He personally delivered a cheque to her home within a day. At the same time I decided not to charge my normal fee. She said, 'It really made a difference, I feel there are people who really care and I'm not alone.'

During one visit I asked Frances what made her feel prosperous? She answered almost immediately, 'Always having flowers in the house and good wine'. Her next budget included these things as essential items. Most of Frances' money went on paying bills. Consequently she rarely had any money in her wallet and often had to turn down invitations from friends. I suggested that she should always carry $50 to help her develop a prosperity consciousness. Whenever she used this money she should replace it immediately.

Six months later, on Christmas Eve, I received a call

from her. It was to relay the good news that she had been given a promotion and with it came a $10 000 a year pay increase. Her spending was under control. She said, 'I just wanted to let you know how wonderful things are. I now know what it's like to feel prosperous. The flowers and wine, plus money in my wallet, made an enormous difference. I no longer feel deprived. There is always money to pay bills when they come in, and for the first time in years, there is money in my savings account if I need it. The most important discovery for me though, is that there are people who care.'

Don't deprive yourself

Notice the words '*I no longer feel deprived*'. Remember that you are a special person and that even the strictest plan must allow for some fun. This idea is contrary to traditional budgets that are based on deprivation. I read a book recently which said that you will never have enough money to achieve your desires, and that in order to get something, you have to give up something. People have been trying this method for years, AND IT DOES NOT WORK. Most of us can do without luxury or fun items for short periods, but how can you acquire wealth if you feel constantly deprived?

The most important thing you can do for yourself and others is to love yourself and one way to do this is to give yourself things you enjoy. It may seem strange to include self-love in a book on money, but working towards riches is counter-productive if you do not like yourself. How can you accumulate riches if secretly you do not believe you deserve them?

Holidays are essential to well-being, and should be considered an investment in yourself. Not everyone has the desire to travel and a week at home can be just as beneficial, provided you pamper yourself. This year, my family and I decided to have a short break at our favourite beach, Shoal Bay. As we have been to this area many times and our activities are restricted by a small baby, I decided to give myself a present every day, such as a facial, massage, hair treatment, visit to chiropractor and so on. After a very uncomfortable pregnancy, it was just what I needed. The cost of my daily presents amounted to $150 over a week. Such an amount is certainly within the reach of most people.

Act rich

When money gets tight the majority of people either cut down on spending or rebel by spending money they don't really have. There is a balance between the two. The last thing you want to do is reinforce a poverty consciousness by acting poor. Expectancy plays an important part, so act rich—dress up, set the table nicely, pick flowers for the house. If there is enough money available, have a manicure or visit the hairdresser. If you are acting prosperously you cannot talk to everyone about how tough things are. It is much better to say nothing. This is not play-acting or burying your head in the sand, it is focusing your attention on what you want.

A natural tendency is to get caught in the trap of treating symptoms of financial problems. Symptoms could be debts, or never having any money left over for you, or could be constantly living beyond your means. One friend of mine has a tendency to overspend on credit cards. Once she's in too deep, she moans about her situation. Then she obtains a consolidation loan, or her father bails her out, and she does the same thing again. Overspending in her situation is a symptom of a deeper problem.

Most people think nothing of consulting a doctor to identify the cause if they are sick, and the same goes for financial problems: it is perfectly natural to ask for help. Help can come from a financial adviser or a counsellor, from a book, or from attending a course. Because money is one of those subjects that people don't talk about readily, it can be difficult to broach the subject, or to ask for help.

Myra's story

Another client gave herself endless anxiety because she was afraid to seek help. My first contact with Myra was on the phone and I noticed how abrupt she was. She was also very tense at our first meeting. For the past twenty years Myra had not lodged a tax return and she lived in fear of being discovered. Finally, overcome by guilt, she confessed, 'I cannot stand it any longer. I realise I may lose my home and even go to jail. Every time I drive past the women's prison I think I'll be in there one day'. When I explained that the worst that could happen was that she would receive a fine, she really didn't believe me.

Another of her problems was that she had barely enough money to live on, although she earned a good salary. She was being taxed at the highest rate because she never had been brave enough to fill in a tax rebate form that would have automatically reduced her tax, as she did not want to alert the Taxation Department to her situation.

It only took minutes to assess that Myra had paid far too much tax and was due for a substantial refund. We could only find records dating back seven years, and the Taxation Department was happy to accept those. The end result was a tax refund of $25 000 and no fine.

It is hard now to believe that this client is the same person. Whereas before she was lucky to have twenty cents in her wallet, she now always carries a reasonable sum of money. She has a new car, new clothes, and a new attitude. Opportunities have arisen for her and it is very possible that she will soon be a wealthy woman.

Make money your slave

As it is virtually impossible to ignore money, make money your slave. Once you master money, it no longer controls you and will lose its importance. It is only when there is not enough, or you fear losing what you have, that you cling to it, worry about it, talk about it and constantly look for solutions. This is misdirected energy which only creates more problems.

Money has a host of myths associated with it: you have to work hard to make money; money only comes through work; there is not enough for everyone; if you have more than your share, then someone else will have to do without; you can't make money being honest; artists, or certain professions have to struggle; it's different for some people; money changes people; rich people are snobs; or, you only get one chance.

If you limit yourself by accepting any of these beliefs then your life will not change. Good fortune may fall into your lap but you will lose it somehow. Desire is the most important ingredient and if you want something badly enough you can achieve it. Prosperity is not just about making lots of money, it is being happy with whatever state you choose.

A mistake that some of my friends and I made when we first started practising positive thinking, was to believe that if we spent and thought positively, the money would come. Sometimes it did, but mostly it did not. You cannot 'fake it till you make it' by living beyond your means and running up debts. This is not acting prosperously, nor does it change the real cause of your problem. By all means act prosperously and pamper yourself, but start living within your means now.

Conclusion

Keeping up with taxation, investments and credit laws is

a full time job, even for those who work at it every day. So don't expect to be an expert on every subject. Never be too embarrassed to ask for help.

Make your own list of items that make you feel prosperous. It need not cost money and should be within your means. If money is limited, join up with someone else to share the cost. In my local baby health centre, there is an advertisement from a young mother wanting to share the cost of a nanny. Two other people share a cleaner, who works for two hours in each home.

Exercise

The following exercise is designed to develop a prosperity consciousness by focusing on the good things in life.

Start a pamper jar. Place in it the cost of a cup of coffee each day, and you will soon have money to spend on yourself.

From your Prosperity List choose one item and give it to yourself regularly. Continually add new items as months go by, but they must be paid for in cash.

Prosperity List

Cleaner	Money readily available
Ironing service	through automatic
Flowers	teller machine
Massage	Money in wallet
Facial	$50/$100/$500
Visit to hairdresser	Investments
Dining out	Doing courses
Good wine	Books
Beautifully set dinner table	Records
Time alone	Starting a collection
Babysitter	Exquisite lingerie
Manicured fingernails	Satin sheets
Clothes	

CHAPTER 2

Uncovering your real beliefs

What do you believe?

Often we think we have a positive attitude towards money but somehow we never seem to achieve our goals. Our life reflects our beliefs. The way we treat money and possessions betrays our hidden beliefs.

For instance, if you long for a luxury sports car, say a Porsche, think how you would treat it. Look at your present car. Do you treat it like a Porsche or a rubbish dump? Is it cleaned and polished, or unwashed and unloved?

How do you treat money? Do you shove it into your wallet any old way, or throw it into a drawer? When a shop assistant gives you change, do you shove it out of sight as quickly as possible? Do you know how much money you have in your wallet? How does this amount make you feel?

The way we treat possessions and the way we dress tells the world what we think about ourselves.

It is extremely difficult to feel and act prosperously if you live in a slum. A slum is not necessarily a derelict neighbourhood; an untidy room can fit the description. Clear away the clutter now, in preparation for the things that you want.

Childhood conditioning

You will also need to clear away the clutter in your mind. You can do this by examining your conditioning—the beliefs and patterns of behaviour established in early childhood. Often, we utter phrases heard and repeated as children, without fully comprehending their significance and impact on our lives.

Do these sound familiar? Money doesn't grow on trees . . . We can't afford it . . . Champagne tastes on a beer income . . . Money is the root of all evil . . . You can't win . . . The rich get richer, the poor get poorer . . . You live beyond your means . . . You're hopeless with money . . . Money burns a hole in your pocket . . . It's greedy to want more than your share . . . You can't make money in business being honest . . . You can't trust anyone . . . Money doesn't bring you happiness.

How many positive phrases about money can you recall? Usually there are very few. Money may not bring happiness, but nor do debts or money worries. In fact money worries rate highly on the list of causes for marriage break-up. Literally hundreds of phrases similar to those mentioned above are a part of our daily life. If you have a problem with money, chances are that your conditioning has been predominantly negative.

As a child, I was told 'You're hopeless with money', because I always spent any change from my lunch or bus money. From the age of eight, I developed a reputation for spending money that was not mine and was continually reminded of it by a well-meaning family. As an adult, I overspent on credit cards and lived beyond my means for many years, repeating the pattern of spending learnt as a child.

Negative reinforcement from parents, teachers and friends makes our weaknesses worse. It's easy to start blaming others for what we are, but we are also part of the process. Listen to what you say to your children, friends, husband and associates: all of us have negative programs that, unwittingly, we pass on to others.

The mind is the most incredible tool but it can work for, or against us. The subconscious mind has no reasoning power and will accept anything—especially emotions—as fact, if it is repeated often enough. Everything that has ever happened to you is remembered.

Negative subconscious beliefs and memories create havoc with our financial affairs. If, as a child, you were told 'we can't afford it', there is a strong likelihood that you have carried that belief with you into adult life, whether or not it holds any truth today. This belief needs to be changed at the subconscious level.

One client whose financial position was very secure said, 'Things cannot get much worse'. Her family always lived a hand-to-mouth existence and although her situation was now entirely different, she was still acting out that old belief.

Conditioning comes not only from the phrases we hear but also from the actions of others, particularly those close to us. My mother belonged to a generation of women who stayed at home and looked after the children. I chose to work, to provide my children and myself with a lifestyle that I found acceptable. Because my mother did not approve, she did not want to hear about my business and my success brought rejection. During tough times, however, she had been incredibly supportive. She would listen, offer money and babysit. Poverty was acceptable; independence was not. Some husbands perpetuate the problem. There are still men who actively discourage their wives from working, because they find the idea of independent women hard to cope with.

Women born prior to the 1960s come from an era where a woman's role was the dependent homemaker. Then came the radical changes of the 60s and women's struggle for equality: suddenly women were expected to contribute financially or to provide for themselves. This pre-60s generation has been caught between two worlds and inner conflict often manifests itself in financial difficulties.

The problem for women is not so much fear of failure but fear of success. Success means throwing away dependency. Although women may appear to be liberated, deep down some are not sure what they want to be.

The real issue in this instance is not money but fear. Fear of change. Fear of success. Fear that you will cease to be loved if you are no longer dependent. My mother said 'No man will ever love you if you are too independent' and, for years I chose the wrong type of man for me, thereby fulfilling her prophecy.

Women who have been taken care of all of their lives suddenly have to face this issue as they get older, if their husband dies, or wants a divorce. They may not have worked for years, or their training is out of date; there are even some who cannot write a cheque. Many believe that they have no purpose any more, that they are innocent victims of circumstance. Is there hope for them? Having helped many such women and seen amazing transformations, my answer is definitely yes. You are never too old; or too poor; or too uneducated.

We all have patterns of behaviour and beliefs that have been shaped by our earliest influences. Don't waste time on blame and recrimination, as it serves no purpose. Simply accept that the beliefs are part of your past.

Dominant seed thoughts

Unlike conditioning which is reinforced by repetition, a dominant seed thought can result from one incident, or one sentence. If you planted any seed in the right conditions it would produce many offspring and the same thing can happen with our memories. An incident that had a large emotional impact on you during the early formative years, could shape your self-image, and affect many of your actions and decisions for years to come.

At one time my life resembled a roller coaster of changing fortunes, one month up, the next down. There was never a blinding flash as to why my life was that way. Self-discovery was for me a gradual process. Seemingly insignificant incidents and small phrases commonly repeated, set my comfort level. Change was like weeding a garden. It took a long time and some of the weeds had very deep roots.

One single incident that affected me happened when I was ten years old. Each of the students at school had to perform in a concert for our class. I chose to sing, and every day leading up to the concert I practised faithfully in front of the bedroom mirror. I thought I was pretty good.

The night before the concert I decided to perform for my family. When I finished I waited expectantly for praise, but instead heard Dad innocently say, 'you're not really going to sing tomorrow, you'll make a fool of yourself'. I was shattered.

The next day I went through the performance again for my class, but this time there was no joy in it. I cringed inwardly but went ahead because I was committed. As far as I can recall, there was no criticism or rejection from the class, but that didn't matter. My father, whom I idolised, thought I was no good, so I mustn't be.

For years afterwards much of my time and energy went into proving myself, although I was not consciously aware of it. Outwardly I appeared confident and spoke positively, but at a deeper level I had a seed thought that said 'I was not good enough'. A remark uttered without thought affected my life for years to come. Whenever something good happened such as making a lot of money, it would be followed by a down period, so that on the whole my financial situation remained the same. I stayed at a level that was within my comfort zone. To perform too well would have meant that my father was wrong.

As adults we can see the folly of such beliefs, but

unfortunately we have no awareness of most of the memories that affect our actions.

As children we have a very strong need to belong and approval from our parents makes us feel important. As we mature, this need to belong does not disappear, but we can transfer it from one person to another. Our partners may replace our parents, but never completely. The need for parental approval seems to remain with us for life. Our work associates and bosses can replace our teachers. As you work through this book you may uncover old thought patterns that you were previously unaware of holding. Be careful though that you do not exchange one set of beliefs for those of your partner or friends. Do not allow your strong sense of belonging to cloud your individual needs. Consciously choose thoughts that will make your life the way you want it to be.

Self-talk

When we are not talking to others, we talk constantly to ourselves. Psychologists estimate that we have 30 000 thoughts a day.

This is such a natural process that we generally do not notice the phrases that circulate in our minds. This self-talk is vitally important. When business started booming for me, I was excited and astounded at how easily it happened and kept repeating 'I don't believe it', until one day I heard myself saying it.

Have you ever said 'It's too good to be true' or 'You can't have it all'? We all use negative phrases and it is essential to be aware of these expressions and, where appropriate, to replace them with more positive ones.

One friend of mine constantly called her daughter 'poor little thing' and did not realise it until I pointed it out. Another always said 'Money goes out faster than it comes in' and almost everyone I know, myself included, has at some stage said 'We can't afford it'.

Some people say these negative expressions are true, that they really can't afford it, but I challenge this. Nine times out of ten, you *choose* to spend money on something else. If you pay a bill instead of going out to dinner, that's a choice. Often parents tell children they can't afford something, but they wouldn't have given them what they asked for anyway. Think carefully before you utter this excuse.

Successful people talk positively to themselves. Instead of saying 'stupid!' when something goes wrong, they say 'I'll do better next time'.

I often call myself brilliant when I come up with a particularly good plan for a client! Not once has a client thought I was conceited; they usually agree and are pleased that I have their best interest in mind. It is always these clients who act on my advice. Would you take the advice of a financial adviser who thought he or she was stupid? Or give a job to someone who said 'I'm a bit dumb, you'll have to explain it to me slowly'. Yet, these phrases are uttered every day.

Our subconscious mind acts like a sponge, soaking up everything it hears without judgement. No wonder so many people experience financial difficulties. Often the throwaway remarks made in casual conversation will betray our real thoughts. For years I simply let these comments wash over me until I decided that my silence did not change anything. Now I usually respond with 'You can win', or, 'You can have it all'. Why not try it?

Questionnaire

AIM: To ascertain how you really feel about money by looking at the way you treat it.

Look in your wallet and see how the notes are placed.
(a) Are they scrunched up, dog-eared, shoved in any old way into numerous compartments?
(b) Are they neat and orderly?

Where do you keep cash?
(a) In the one place, say a wallet or drawer?
(b) Do you throw it into the bottom of your handbag, or scatter it about the house?

How many bank accounts do you have?
(a) A few, each with a special purpose.
(b) Umpteen different accounts, for no particular reason at all.

Do you know how much money you have?
(a) In your wallet.
(b) In the bank.

How do you treat possessions?
(a) With care.
(b) Lose interest once you've had them for a while.

How do you treat your present car?
(a) The way you would treat a luxury car?
(b) Or as a rubbish dump?

How do you talk about money?
(a) Constantly moan about how little there is.
(b) Rarely talk about it.
(c) Always talk positively.

Exercise

Write down as many negative phrases about money as
you can remember.

Champagne Tastes on a Beggars wage

In one ear and out the other, Just like your dad

Where did you hear them?

Family   friends

Colleagues.

For the next seven days make a note of the things you
say about money, whether in your head or aloud. If you
have a non-judgemental friend or family member ask them
to help you.

Choose one constantly-used negative phrase to work
on at a time, and replace it with a new positive one. For
instance, replace, 'With my luck' with 'Things always work
out for me'. Rather than 'I can't afford it' say 'I'll spend
my money on something else'.

CHAPTER 3

What do you really want?

Before making any recommendations on investments or savings plans for clients I always try to assess the personality of the clients. At the same time, I try to discover their real dreams, which is not always easy, as people will often say what is expected of them.

A standard question I used to ask was 'What are your goals?'. The answers I received were understandably varied. Some people did not know what they wanted, or were afraid to say. When I asked these same people what lifestyle they wanted to lead, everyone knew the answer.

Wanting is natural and right. Every single thing started with an idea: a business, an image, a building, this book. At one time they were only ideas in someone's mind.

We limit ourselves, restricting what we can have by aiming for what is expected of us, or placing limitations upon ourselves. Forget shoulds, forget goals even. What are your dreams? If you prefer to travel the world rather than buy a home, consider it seriously. But don't rule out the possibility of having both, if that is what you really want. A frequent comment is, 'I've never really thought about what I want; no-one has ever asked me'. It's easy to get caught in the survival trap, doing what is expected and aiming for what you are supposed to have. Don't be embarrassed to say what you really want.

Cynthia's flatmate was moving out and rather than search for a new apartment or someone to share with, Cynthia wanted to buy a place of her own. She had a good salary, but only a few thousand in the bank. Rather timidly Cynthia approached me for help.

She started talking about her goals two to three years into the future, which did not solve her immediate problem. When I asked 'But what do you really want now?' she immediately responded 'My own apartment within two months'. Her goal was finally out in the open and we could plan accordingly.

We calculated how much Cynthia could borrow, and it was less than the price she had in mind. She agreed to keep an open mind and look at what she could afford now. Two weeks later she rang and said 'I found it'. Everything fell into place and Cynthia was able to move in within the two months she had set herself.

'It's like a dream come true, I didn't really think I could have it. You made it all so simple.' I simply gave Cynthia permission to have what she really wanted, and because I am the so-called expert it was acceptable.

Often clients ring just for reassurance, to have someone say it is O.K. for them to have their heart's desire. Find someone in your life who will support your dreams.

A word of caution: saying what you really want is fine, but be careful whom you share it with. Most people are only too happy to tell you what you cannot have.

What does money represent to you?

Sometimes a client will say to me 'I want to accumulate a lot of money'. It's totally acceptable to want money for security, or status, or just to have available for unexpected opportunities. Generally though, it is difficult to maintain enthusiasm for something so nebulous. Insurance statistics show that the average savings plan originally taken over a ten, twenty or thirty year period, has a life expectancy of less than seven years. Specific goals such as a holiday or a house are easier to visualise and, therefore, to mentally accept. Keep an open mind, do not rule out ideas simply because they seem out of reach.

How many people live the life they believe they should lead? Locked into careers, marriages, or homes by financial commitments, they do not even contemplate alternatives. One friend of mine, an executive with an international company, commented that he would love to be a landscape gardener. Having known this person for nearly twenty years I was stunned. He won't even contemplate such a change because he is committed financially to a certain lifestyle. If he took the time to examine what he really wants, he may find that he prefers his current position. As it is, he will go through life always feeling unfulfilled.

'orget the 'how' and just concentrate on what you really wa it. What would you choose if life was a hobby?

Achievers don't get bogged down in discovering ways to reach goals, they simply focus on what they want. Once a goal is accepted as reality in your mind, it is simply a matter of time before it manifests itself, as long as you take action when necessary.

Planning

Life does not stand still. Either you decide where you want to go, or events and other people will carry you along and you may not like where you end up. A plan does not have to be a complicated or detailed list of procedures. In some cases it can be extremely simple.

I had always had a vague idea that I would like to write one day, but it was a very indefinite sort of goal. Not long after I started working in my present job this goal became clearer when I decided that a column on money matters was a good way to start. I set a time limit of six months to achieve this aim. My plan was to use the laws of attraction by visualising my name and photo on the top of all columns I read. That was all.

A couple of months passed and I met two journalists. One asked me to write an article for a business magazine. It was published. The second journalist mentioned that the magazine she worked for needed a financial columnist. I followed up by submitting material to the editor. Within six months I was writing for two magazines and two newspapers.

Some may say it was connections, but let's examine the facts. Before becoming a financial adviser, I knew no journalists. I had no experience at writing, nor had I done any writing courses. My thought, once it became specific, was magnetic and attracted the right people to assist me. Then I took the necessary action when opportunity came along. That is vital. You can attract opportunities to you, but you must follow through.

There are times when it is essential to obtain the necessary qualification. You cannot be a doctor or a lawyer, without many years of study and a degree. I could not advise on investments without studying, becoming licensed and attending on-going training sessions.

If you are not prepared, or lack the resources to obtain a qualification, check out alternatives that will fulfil your aims. One girl I know loves flying and to her, the best part of any holiday is the plane trip. She would love to be a pilot, but is not prepared to put in the study or money to achieve this dream. She decided that being a flight attendant was the best choice for her. Another woman I know wanted to be a commercial pilot, in the days when women pilots were excluded by the airlines. She obtained her pilot's licence for pleasure and became an air traffic controller instead.

Aiming too high too soon is a common reason for failure. This can be overcome by breaking all goals down into small components. Nearly every goal can be broken down, making it more acceptable to the conscious mind.

Do whatever groundwork is necessary so that you can act without delay when opportunity comes. If you are serious about achieving your dreams you must be prepared.

Another trap that many of us fall into is the false belief that we have to work hard to be wealthy, or that we must stay in a job that is dull and boring because it provides security. Prosperous people work smart. Whilst I believe there may be times when we all have to do something we don't really want to for a time, it does not have to stay that way. Looking back, there have been times when I have worked extremely hard and progressed very little. The occasions when I have achieved goals easily have been when I have been very clear on what I wanted, and refused to accept anything less.

If your goal is for peace of mind and a comfortable lifestyle, aim for that and don't be persuaded that you should aim for more. KNOW WHAT YOU WANT AND REFUSE TO ACCEPT ANYTHING LESS. Ultimately you will get what you want if you are persistent.

Self-directed or other-directed

People with high self-esteem make their own choices. They are in control. They look at the options, the consequences and then make decisions. They take personal responsibility for their lives and do not blame their situation on circumstances or other people.

Other-directed people function out of the belief that they have no control, no choices. They believe they have to live up to someone else's image or expectations. Other-directed people either comply, therefore building up resentment and anger, or they rebel.

A common example is someone who is unhappy in a job. The job pays well and the person has responsibilities, so cannot leave easily.

A self-directed person would say 'O.K. I accept that I don't like this job but I am prepared to make the most of it while I am here. Meanwhile I will keep looking for something more suitable'. This person makes the choice to stay on to avoid the consequence of being unemployed, but takes positive action by looking for an alternative.

Other-directed people constantly moan about their jobs and how miserable they are. They would say something like this, 'I hate this job, it is so boring and the people are horrible. Every morning I wake up and dread the day ahead, but what can I do? I have a family to support, commitments, I can't just walk away like some people. Someone has to be responsible.' So they remain, often for years, because people acting out of this belief think they have no choices.

Same situation, different attitude. You do not need a degree in psychology to see who would easily attract a new job. Opportunities gravitate to confident and cheerful people who know what they want.

It's O.K. to change your mind

Be flexible as you grow and learn more about yourself. It is natural that some goals will change, along the way. You may not want a lot of money as much as the lifestyle such money would bring, so there may be another way to achieve your desired way of life.

If in doubt as to what you want, ask questions of yourself and of others. For instance, many people fall into a career because they don't really know what they want to do. Years later they find they are stuck in the same career, often still undecided. In today's society a career change in your thirties, forties, and even sixties is possible. When you make work a hobby, then you never want to retire. During my search for a career change I went to a career planning consultant and found the advice invaluable. If you don't know what type of work you want to do, research what professional advice is available and make decisions about little things. For instance, do you want to work indoors or outdoors? What type of environment do you want to work in? What type of people do you want to work with? Do you want to work in the city or suburbs? What hours do you want to work? These seemingly insignificant decisions will immediately rule out certain choices and will eventually present you with a very clear picture of what is right for you.

Don't rush in and commit yourself to long-term study, unless you are sure that it will lead to what you really want. When I sold one business and before starting in my present career, I considered working in public relations, personnel, accounting and publishing, before finding my niche in investments. Rather than waste my time studying various subjects, I researched these careers by talking to people already working in them. At one time, I joined an Association and went along to its functions, only to find that this area of work was not for me.

Are your goals in conflict? Many women are torn between their home and family obligations and the desire for a career. While you may choose to put your dreams to one side for now, don't leave them there forever. Consider compromise—there may be an alternative.

When Jenny discovered she was pregnant, she sold her business to become a full-time mother. Two years later she found that she was restless, although her desire to be with her child had not changed. At the same time, I wanted to expand my business, without working longer hours. As the result of a casual conversation, we found a way to achieve both our goals.

Jenny is now licensed to conduct my 'Financially Free' course as her own business. She is able to work nights and Saturday afternoons, when her husband is available to spend time with their child. She decides how often she wants to work and when, and the added bonus is that she has extra money and feels more fulfilled. I've also achieved my goal to expand my business. By training more women like Jenny, I'm able to reach more people, but still have more time to spend with my baby.

Never settle for mediocrity, you can have it all if you are prepared to work for it. For it is you and no-one else who decides what your life will be.

Shared dreams

While dreams are generally personal there will be times when you might share a goal with a husband, wife, business partner, friend or employer. We all perceive things differently and while we may think we are headed in the same direction, lack of explicit communication can totally ruin the best plans.

John and Celia are typical of many married couples who thought they shared the same goal. To achieve his goal of a salary of $100 000 a year, John had to reach a certain rank in his company. That meant putting in extra hours at work and being available for social functions and travel. Celia, left at home looking after their three children, was not included in her husband's working life. She hardly saw him and gradually resentment built up. Eventually they became two people living together with nothing in common any more. When their marriage reached a crisis point, John said 'Well, I'm doing it for you. You want the lifestyle, so put up with it'.

We can start off with the same goal yet often the reality is different to what we imagined. This is usually because two people see two different pictures of the same thing. Business partnerships have a notoriously high rate of breakdown for this very reason. One partner sees his own business as freedom to work less, the other believes that he has to work long hours for the first few years. Different belief systems. No wonder they don't succeed. The energies that each partner originally focused on a mutual goal are now directed to the frustrations, resentment and problems that have developed. Certainly not an atmosphere conducive to success.

Naomi Eyers, lead singer with the Fabulous Singlettes encountered this problem with her original singing group. 'Our first booking for the Singlets was for three weeks. We had no plans to take the act beyond that time. The booking was extended and soon we had offers to play all over the country. Two of the girls who were a part of the original trio did not have such high expectations, nor did they want to travel overseas. Eventually they left and had to be replaced. For a while I thought there was something wrong with me.'

It was at this time that Naomi attended her first 'Financially Free' course, and undertook an exercise set out in the course for people sharing goals. Naomi directed her efforts towards looking for replacement singers with similar goals. 'Once we found them, everything fell into place. The act is now better than the original one because we are all working towards a common goal.' The group has since gone from strength to strength and has achieved success in Australia and overseas.

How long has it been since you and your partner have compared goals? After the initial enthusiasm for a project has died down we forget to check what the other person thinks and feels. We assume. Assumption is a silent killer of any relationship. We can never be one hundred per cent sure of what is going on in someone else's mind, no matter how well we know that person. We do not have the right to make decisions for other people. People change, dreams change. Everyone who shares a goal needs to communicate on a regular basis.

What is your purpose in life?

There has to be an overriding reason for living, a purpose for each one of us, otherwise we would not survive the tough times, nor have the incentive to aim for the stars.

Have you ever thought what your purpose in life may be? The easiest way I have found to do this is to imagine that you are aged 90 and reflecting on the life you have lived. What would you have liked to achieve? Do you have any regrets? What is important to you?

I ask participants in my workshops: What unique qualities do you have? How do you enjoy using these qualities? Responses are naturally varied. Some people want to grow spiritually, emotionally; to help others; to help their children; to be the best they can. Never have I heard anyone say that their purpose in life is to make a lot of money. Money seems to be a by-product of success.

I took my baby Laura to the beach for the first time when she was four months old. Although she was unable to sit alone, she lay on the beach mat and chuckled as she gazed around her. I marvelled at her delight over something we consider enjoyable, but commonplace. What a wonderful purpose in life, simply to enjoy being. In the process she adds sunshine to countless lives along the way.

There have been many stories told of prisoners-of-war who survived simply because they had a purpose. For some it was revenge, for others it was to get back to their families. Despite unimaginable hardship, the prisoners with a purpose survived against incredible odds, whilst others with better conditions, yet no purpose, did not.

A purpose is your reason for living. It can be a powerful motivational force for achieving your goals.

Exercise

AIM: The purpose of this exercise is to prepare you for when opportunity comes.

Contemplate the life you would lead if money were no object.

What type of home would you live in?

_____

_____

_____

Who would you live with?

_____

_____

_____

Where would you live?

_____

_____

_____

What work would you do?

_____

_____

_____

What would you do with your leisure time?

_____

_____

Who would you share your leisure time with?

_____

_____

What would you look like?

_____

_____

Take your time and really think about what you want your life to be. If unsure, do some research. If you don't know the type of home you want, or area you want to live in, inspect houses that are for sale, even those out of your price range.

Do you need additional skills or training? Check out what courses are available.

Think about your purpose in life. Are your goals compatible with this purpose?

Set priorities. What is most important to you now?

Allow your decision about what you want from life to be a personal choice, not something that is forced upon you.

Accept that there may be times when you may choose to put a dream on hold.

Exercise: shared goals

AIM: To ensure that all parties to a goal are headed in the same direction.

Ask all parties involved to complete this exercise separately.

List all that you can about your common goal. Be specific as to what you want from it; money, location, time priorities, lifestyle.

_____

_____

_____

Where does this goal rate in comparison to other goals you may have?

_____

_____

_____

Define the purpose of this goal?

_____

_____

_____

Check your list against that of your partner. Are they complementary?

_____

_____

_____

Differences are natural and may be unimportant; others may necessitate some compromise.

Try to do this exercise once a year to ensure that you both continue in the same direction.

CHAPTER 4

Become the person you want to be

Raise your comfort level

Imagine that you could instantly have everything you wanted. The money, car, house, or holiday you've dreamed of. No more money worries, what bliss! Or would it be? Every week some people are that lucky when they become instant millionaires by winning lotteries, pools, lotto. Statistics show that four out of five pools' winners revert to their original state within five years. Why? Because this new state does not fit their self-image.

Within each of us is a very detailed picture of the person that we think we are. This image encompasses our appearance, skills, wealth, intelligence, and sets our comfort zone.

This picture is only how you perceive yourself. It may not necessarily be the real you, but you will make it true by your actions. You cannot change this picture by sheer willpower, only by reprogramming your mental computer. People who think they are ordinary, or average, will have difficulty accepting wealth if it is suddenly thrust upon them—no matter how much it was desired.

One of my clients was about to inherit some money and I suggested she use part of this inheritance to purchase a holiday home. Although she would still have plenty of money left, she looked aghast and said 'You mean I can really have a holiday home? I would love it, but that's for other people, not people like me. It will take a while for me to accept it'. She was right—she will have to change her self-image if she wants to avoid sabotaging herself.

Who are you? Are you the person you want to be, or is your self-image tied to the roles you play? Some of the roles women play are wife, mother, dependent child, career woman, teacher, friend, lover, victim, rescuer, or maybe just superwoman.

Rebecca was used to struggling and having no money. When her divorce was finalised she received a settlement of $30 000 from her ex-husband. At first she placed this money in the bank, but when the tax bill came in, she decided to seek advice on some alternative investments. That was when I first met her. Recommending investments was relatively simple, but Rebecca needed more time to make up her mind.

Three months later she returned to see me, seeking the same advice, but still needing more time to make a decision. As she was leaving my office she said 'I wish I didn't have this money, it's more trouble than its worth'. I knew then that she would sabotage herself.

Twelve months passed and Rebecca rang again. This time she said 'Wasn't it lucky I didn't invest the money, because I really needed it'. Her car had been demolished in an accident. Normally it was insured, but this time it was not. She had also changed from full-time employment to part-time, while she thought about the work she would like to do. Within two years Rebecca had no money left and was back to her comfort level.

Changing your self-image

You can begin to change your self image by acting like the person you want to be. Dress is the easiest place to start. Do you dress the part of a successful person? When I go to the office to see clients I have a certain standard of dress, but since my baby was born I've chosen to work more from home. I don't wear my office clothes at home because with a baby it would be neither practical nor comfortable. But I do not wear the same clothes I would do the gardening in either. I just cannot feel successful and prosperous in jeans and sloppy joe. So I have had to adapt my wardrobe to include clothes that are comfortable and serviceable, yet acceptable to my self-image.

Some images are not as simple as changing the way you look. If your self-image is one of being a failure then you need to do something to change it. Affirmations such as 'I'm successful' are not always enough. Build little successes, dress up at home, do a course, but make sure it is short enough to finish, save regularly, even if it's $2 a week, attend a self-esteem workshop. It doesn't matter what it is, provided that it is relevant to the image you want to create.

The images that you hold may vary for different aspects of your life. You may think and act as an intelligent and successful person at work, but have a belief that you are hopeless with money. So you need to do something to change that belief. You could do this by learning more about money management and investments; by reorganising your records, so that you know exactly how much you earn and where it goes; by paying bills on time; or contacting creditors if you are unable to pay and coming to an arrangement with them about discharging your debts.

Expectancy

What you expect is what you get. Expect life to be a struggle, not enough to go around, and it will be. Expect to have money, or that everything will work out, and it will.

Fortunately people with high expectations who lose money, quickly return to their original condition as well.

Mary went on a spending spree not long after her husband died. 'At first I felt so lost that whenever I felt like it, I would hop on a plane to see my daughter in Melbourne. Then I would go to see my son in New Zealand. We always lived well and as my husband had always looked after our finances, I never thought much about money. After twelve months spent renovating the house, taking numerous trips, buying the children and grandchildren presents, I realised I'd spent most of my capital.'

Mary had to cut down on her lifestyle considerably and thought she would have to apply for the old age pension. Before I even had time to prepare a financial plan for Mary, she was offered a part-time job. Her daughter moved home and helped share the expenses. Shortly afterwards Mary inherited a large some of money from an unexpected source. This allowed her to return to a level at which she felt comfortable.

This might just seem to be coincidence, but I have seen people with high expectations attract countless opportunities. Our level of expectation has a lot to do with our success. Set your expectations too high, too soon, and you will rarely achieve them. Your internal success barometer will quickly sabotage you. Set your expectations too low, and your life will remain unchanged.

On a recent holiday, my daughter observed two dress shops. Both were within metres of each other, both in arcades, although one store had a slightly better position. One store was prospering, while the other appeared to be barely surviving. Lisa had no trouble seeing why, although her only experience at marketing comes from being a consumer.

The unsuccessful store had little stock and throughout the week, neither window display nor stock changed. During Lisa's visit, the shop assistant was on the phone moaning about how bad business was, commenting that they made only $16 on a Saturday during school holidays. Lisa commented later that as they had nothing that was worthwhile and the atmosphere was depressing, she did not feel like returning.

The second store opened seven days a week and every time we passed, it was full of people, although it was low season when we were there. They had an extensive range of sizes and styles, from teenagers to grandmothers. Neither Lisa nor I had any intention of buying any clothes or accessories, but they changed the window display twice a day, and it was so interesting that we could not resist going in. In fact we went into that shop at least once a day for a week and consequently bought a swimsuit, tops, business suit, plus numerous accessories.

The difference between the two stores comes down to expectancy. The first shopkeeper did not expect to be successful and sat around moaning. She may not have had as much money but she could have changed her window display, moved stock around, any number of little tricks to make people want to buy her goods. A positive expectancy is essential for success. The belief comes first, success follows. Practical knowledge helps but without a positive attitude you will rarely succeed.

Recently I attended a fashion parade in a dressmaker's home. Two young women were attempting to start a business designing their own range of women's clothing. They explained that this was their first parade and if it was successful, they would hold others. The whole event was rather unprofessional, but like most of the people there, I was prepared to overlook this aspect of it.

What astounded me was their lack of expectancy—they did not expect to succeed. How do I know? Because they did not advertise their name, address or phone number all evening. As I was invited by a friend, who in turn was invited by someone at work, I did not know their names, and the suburb was out of my area, so it is unlikely that I would find the house again. They did not ask my name and address. They had no business cards, no leaflets and receipts issued had no name or phone number on them.

Their range of clothing could only be obtained from them and I checked quite thoroughly on labels and display racks and there was no contact name or number. They went to so much trouble, put on a beautiful supper, made heaps of clothes, opened their home and neglected the most important point.

To reach your ultimate goal of being financially free, continually raise your expectations, but take care each time not to exceed what you can mentally accept. For instance, if you want a salary of $50 000 a year and currently receive $20 000, aim for $30 000 a year, and once you've achieved this aim for $35 000 a year. If your current position will not pay this much, look at another job, or alternative ways to make money.

If you find it difficult to spend money on yourself, buy something extravagant once a month, that you would not normally buy. You cannot expand your comfort level without making changes to your pattern of saving and spending. Once you accept any goal as reality in your mind, it is only a matter of time before it presents itself.

Taking personal responsibility

When we take responsibility for our lives, we cease to blame other people or circumstances for where we are today.

Do you know a victim? Everything goes wrong for the victims. They live in a state of perpetual misery and just when things appear to be improving something else goes wrong. They lose their jobs; have accidents; have their cars stolen; become sick; or get ripped off. They create one disaster after another. Being a victim gains them a lot of attention, and keeps them safe from change.

Jan is a chronic victim. When I first met her she was selling off items of furniture just to pay bills. She sold her microwave to pay for her first visit to me. In a few short months Jan managed to spend her entire divorce settlement and run up huge debts as well—the repayments were beyond her means.

Solutions such as a consolidation loan were out of the question as she was overcommitted and a bad credit risk. We assessed the obvious solutions: share accommodation, a second job, a higher paying job, bankruptcy. Solutions were short-lived, because Jan was a master saboteur and as soon as conditions improved, she changed jobs. It appeared to be a good move, with a hefty pay increase and the opportunity for overtime. However, her new employer's reputation was unsavoury and most people knew it. He couldn't always cover wages, the Taxation Department was investigating him, the media was hounding him and finally he was declared bankrupt.

'Why me?' became a familiar lament. A new job was followed by an eviction notice and panic-stricken Jan grabbed the first opportunity to share accommodation. Weeks after moving in, her new housemate committed suicide and Jan had to move again.

This time she decided to move interstate and live with her widowed mother until the debts were clear. This arrangement only lasted weeks. She moved again . . . .more removalists bills . . . .her new housemate turned out to be psychotic and threatened to kill her. She moved again and is now finding difficulty obtaining a job. She said 'I think some devil spirit is following me around'. Changing jobs, houses and husbands doesn't work, because we take our self with us. Jan's worst enemy is herself. She gains constant attention from her troubles, and this is the payoff for her. As this happens on a subconscious level, most victims are unaware of the role they are playing.

Jan has a sense of humour and can laugh at her troubles. She has a talent for turning a difficult situation into something comic. She has two options: she can turn her problems into an opportunity, possibly by becoming a comedy writer; or, she can stop talking about her troubles, thereby negating the attention she gains from them. When she no longer gains sympathy from her troubles, she can find positive ways to gain recognition and the problems will resolve themselves.

What are you gaining?

For every victim there is a rescuer, the person who always has a solution for everyone else's problems. Rescuers often complain that there is never any time, they are so busy running around helping everyone else. They are often very caring people, but they feel that they have to save the world, and have trouble saying no. They put everyone else's needs before their own, but there is a payoff for them too, in not having sufficient time to solve their own problems.

Ruth, an accountant, provided a service to busy executives who could not manage their own financial affairs. Often, these people would run up huge debts, and overcommit to mortgages. Because of their position in the community, they could not afford the embarrassment of cheques bouncing, or credit being rejected. So, for a hefty fee, Ruth took over managing their money completely. She started by taking charge of their cheque book and credit cards. She negotiated with creditors, paid all bills and allocated these clients a weekly allowance. At first I thought it was a great idea, and referred some clients to her. It wasn't long before my clients and I discovered that taking over responsibility for someone else does not work, because this system never addresses the real problem of why the person overspends, nor does it teach them coping skills, or ways to change their habits. In the case of one client, all she incurred was an additional debt of $5000, for this management service. When she couldn't afford to pay this either, she was forced to take over her own affairs again, without acquiring any new money management skills, nor ways to cope with her compulsive spending. Businesses such as this are merely acting as rescuers.

Most of us have been both victim and rescuer at times. Don't feel bad about it; learning the games that we play is part of personal development. Reformed rescuers like me write self-help books or run seminars. Find a constructive way to use your energies and you get the love and attention you deserve.

Always having mum, dad, husband or friend available to constantly bail you out of financial difficulties allows you to remain dependent. There is nothing wrong with giving or receiving, if the giving is unconditional, but if the motive of the giver is to support dependency, then it benefits no-one.

Getting even is another motive. Take a woman whose husband has left her. If she wants to make him pay, she will often take on the role of the victim, to support her belief that she was the injured party. Financial difficulties can be a form of revenge.

Having no money means that you cannot take a risk and try something new. If you did try and bettered your husband or parents you may encounter problems that you don't want. Having no money keeps you safe from failure, success, change or making a fool of yourself, and it keeps you safe from taking responsibility.

There is nothing wrong with staying in any situation as long as you realise that it is a personal choice and that you gain from being there. Give yourself permission to change at your own pace. Being responsible does not mean becoming a rescuer and it is not a burden or a duty.

All of us are only responsible for ourselves and for our children, until they are old enough to take over for themselves. Love means supporting, encouraging, but not taking over or taking reponsibility for anyone else's happiness. When you can accept this you realise that no longer is the government, boss, family, husband, child or friend responsible for conditions in your life. You are. This brings an enormous sense of liberation. The wonderful benefit of freedom of choice is that we may discover that we have what we really wanted all along.

One client of mine returned to work after thirty years, when her marriage broke up. For ten years she hated the daily grind of going to the office and longed for the day when she could afford to retire. When she inherited some money she was at last free to leave. She discovered then that she liked her job and decided to stay on. Emotions such as anger, resentment or hurt feelings are the real barriers to prosperity, not conditions or other people.

You may not have wanted to be unemployed; have a husband die or leave; lose money; become ill. It is your reaction to such events and subsequent action that is a matter of choice. We gain something from every situation, be it positive or negative. Jean Nidetch, the founder of Weight Watchers, could have remained fat all her life, but she found a solution that worked for her and decided to share it with others. In the process she founded a multi-million dollar business that helps people all over the world.

There are hundreds of excuses we all use because we are not ready to change yet. Don't concentrate on the payoff, or the situation. Do concentrate on what you would like your life to be. Work at changing your beliefs, raising your expectancy and automatically you will let go of any payoffs. Your mind can only really focus on one thought at a time so it may as well be on what you want.

Love yourself first

Most of us were taught to put others first, but you cannot give to another what you cannot give to yourself. The most important thing you can do is to love yourself unconditionally. From that everything else follows.

It is that one word UNCONDITIONAL that makes the difference. It is easy to love yourself when everything is going right. But what about when you put on weight, lose a job, fail an exam, or run up debts? Yet that is the time when you need to love yourself the most.

A friend of mine is a wonderful person, with all the qualities of a winner. He's intelligent, dedicated, quick-thinking as well as warm, caring and charming. In his career and relationships he is successful to a point, but has never reached the level he aimed for, although he has had many opportunities. Something always manages to sabotage him whenever success is imminent. He freely admits that he does not like himself. He often puts himself down and has difficulty accepting a compliment.

This point of self-love has confused some students in my course. People have said to me 'Well what do you really mean by love myself? Of course I think I do, but how do I know?'

If you are not sure, then you do not love yourself unconditionally. Self-love means knowing that you deserve the best from life; that you like yourself all the time. You may not always like your actions, but your actions are not you. It's being able to accept a compliment graciously. It's being able to look yourself in a mirror and say to yourself 'I love you'. Putting yourself first does not mean putting other people down, nor is it an excuse for bad manners. It should not be confused with selfishness.

The world around us acts as a giant mirror and the reflection that we receive from others mirrors the aspects of our personality that we like or dislike. As you learn to love yourself, you will receive love back from others. As you raise your level of expectancy, people, jobs and opportunities, will reflect this new attitude. When I first began advising on money matters I attracted clients with only small amounts of money. Nowadays I attract clients with very large sums.

I can easily tell how I am feeling by looking at my appointment book. If a number of clients procrastinate, I look to my own life to see where I am procrastinating.

If you are having fear and insecurity mirrored back from someone close to you, check if there is something that makes you feel insecure.

What can you do about it?

Look at the people in your life. Are they the way you want to be? Like attracts like and when you feel prosperous, positive and confident you attract like-minded people to you. That is why people who are comfortable with themselves seem to effortlessly attract success, money and people to them. The old saying that 'money makes money' could also be 'money attracts money'.

In his book on champion marathon runner Robert de Castella,[1] author Mike Jenkinson says 'It is remarkable how the right people have always been on hand to fill vital roles in Rob's running life'. Success or prosperity do not have to be achieved alone, as the right people will invariably come along to assist you. That is the real truth about being in the right place at the right time and luck plays no part.

If everything goes wrong, everyone criticises you and you never have enough money, chances are that you secretly don't like yourself very much. Try loving yourself instead, and watch things change.

You can start by saying to yourself each day 'I love you (name)'. Don't wait for someone else to tell you. Say it in front of a mirror and take note of your reaction, but it is generally a good idea to make sure that you are alone. I suggested this exercise to one client, and she was astounded. She said 'I really believed that I loved myself and deserved to be prosperous. But when I tried to say it in front of a mirror, I stuttered. I just couldn't look myself in the eye and lie'.

Give yourself presents. It doesn't have to be something that costs money. It could be time alone, a bubble bath, or anything that you enjoy. Treat yourself the way you want others to treat you. People who say they want money to help others are either playing the rescuer, or believe they don't deserve it for themselves.

You cannot wait until you make your fortune, find the perfect partner, or succeed in business, to love yourself. To do so would be putting your life on hold forever. You need to love the whole person, both the weak and strong parts of your personality.

Sub-personalities

As Jan got on the train to travel home from work, her whole mood changed from being happy and confident to being depressed. Jan is an executive secretary and good at her job. She could not understand how her home and work life could be in such contrast. At work she is surrounded by luxury and lots of people and she is successful. At home, she lived alone in stark conditions and felt a failure.

Within each person there are many different personalities that make up the whole person. Jan's workplace reflected the positive feelings she held about herself at work, yet the person she was away from work was unacceptable to her. Her home, debts and general lifestyle reflected this.

There can be hundreds of sub-personalities and no matter how mature or well-balanced you are, there will be times when the child within you will emerge. For instance, when a parent dies, you can forget that you are a capable adult and feel like a small, hurt, lost child.

You may love the side of you that is a good parent, friend, or loyal partner, or the part of you that is prepared to take risks. You may reject the insecure, vulnerable, dependent side of yourself. If you relinquish control you allow the parts that you do not particularly like to dominate and control your life, which happens when you focus too much on your weaknesses. The positive alternative is to choose to love the whole person and work on strengthening the unacceptable parts.

Acceptance of yourself as you are this minute is vital.

You can never love anyone else more than you love yourself. Most of us look to someone else for acceptance, believing that if only someone would love us, or our parents would approve of us, then everything would be all right. Acceptance is not outside of you, it comes from within. Your own approval is all that you need.

Give yourself permission to be less than perfect. You can do this by affirming 'I love my insecurity' or 'I love my poverty', or whatever is appropriate. You may not feel any different at first, but the willingness to accept all of you will swing the pendulum in your favour. Eventually you will feel more comfortable about being poor, or in debt, or fearful. When you cease resisting, then circumstances often change of their own accord.

If you gain something from every situation, then what appears to be negative is really doing something positive for you. You may not be ready to change, or face a fear. Our minds have an inbuilt defence mechanism and your defences may be there for a good reason. So don't berate yourself for being less than perfect.

What does your body tell you?

How you feel about yourself also reflects in your body and in the way you talk, walk and feel and no amount of acting can hide this. Imagine yourself walking, running or doing any physical activity and the muscles work in the same way as if you were actually doing it. Your mind cannot tell the difference between what is real and what is vividly imagined.

Emotions such as anger, resentment, hurt feelings, excitement and joy need to be released. If they are not, this energy becomes trapped in the body and can result in physical ailments. We've all heard comments such as ' . . . is a pain in the neck', ' . . . gives me a headache', or, 'I feel weighed down with responsibilities'. Often people who use these expressions develop stiff neck, headache, shoulder and back pain or a weight problem.

Louise Hay, author of *You Can Heal Your Life* lists many of the physical ailments that relate to mental conditions. I have found that they are extremely accurate. Next time you get the flu or have a backache, check what is going on in your life.

For example Louise Hay suggests that asthma could be related to feeling stifled and that back pain relates to various problems including lack of emotional support, guilt and fear of money. She believes that high blood pressure can result from prolonged emotional problems and that low blood pressure may arise from a sense of defeatism or insufficient love as a child.

Hay links headaches to self criticism, indigestion to anxiety, flu to fear and bronchitis to difficulties in the family situation.[2]

These are but a few. Find ways to express your emotions appropriately. Exercise is a wonderful outlet; writing everything down helps; scream if you have to. There are also many alternative therapies such as massage, deep tissue therapy, acupuncture and kinesiology, that all work on releasing blocked energy. As well as providing therapeutic benefits, these treatments can be an enjoyable experience.

It's O.K. to feel angry

Children are sometimes punished for throwing tantrums or hitting a parent. Have you ever seen a parent tower over a tiny child and say 'Don't you get angry with me'? If you imagine it from the child's perspective, it can be quite frightening. So, from an early age, we learn that acceptance means that certain feelings such as anger, selfishness, greed are considered BAD.

Emotions by themselves are not bad, even the supposedly negative ones. Think about that for a moment. What is wrong with feeling angry? There have been many times when anger has been a catalyst for change when levelled at injustice, at governments, at big corporations polluting the atmosphere. Emotions by themselves are neither good nor bad, but the actions resulting from these feelings can be expressed in detrimental or unhelpful ways. It helps no-one to vent anger by spending the family savings, breaking every bit of china in the house, going on an eating binge, or bashing someone. So, as a general rule, we have learnt to suppress unacceptable emotions, or to ignore them in the hope that they will go away. The trouble is, they never do.

Learn appropriate ways of expressing your feelings and recognise and accept that every day of your life is not going to be perfect. Some days I feel depressed. I have learnt to allow myself to have a down day every now and then and by accepting the feeling, it quickly passes. Sometimes other people say, cheer up, look on the bright side, be positive. At times these comments help, but mostly they confirm that only positive behaviour is acceptable. Finding one person that you can be totally yourself with, someone who accepts your highs and lows, is immensely freeing.

There will be times when emotions have to be suppressed because the time is not right or the feelings are too difficult to handle. Try to find ways to deal with troublesome emotions as they arise. Be gentle with yourself. It takes time to acquire a new habit.

There is no blame

As human beings we all make mistakes, often unknowingly. I overheard some grandparents admonishing their five-year-old grandson. Their conversation went as follows: 'Stupid child, I knew you would knock that over. Sit up straight, don't slouch. Don't do that, you'll get into trouble. Here come the police to get you.' I felt rather sorry for the little boy who seemed to be a quite normal lively child. It would be so easy to judge these people for being so critical, but haven't we all done it at some time? Maybe these grandparents resented minding the child, they may have been sick, or believed that by criticising him they were teaching him good manners, possibly they had problems of their own. Who knows?

We all need to forgive someone, the boss who didn't give you the promotion, the woman at work who drives you mad, the husband who left you, the children who spend all your money, the friend who was not there when you needed her. The list goes on, but the first person on your list should be yourself. Forgiving can be incredibly powerful, it releases pent up emotions that keep you from moving forward. It can also be very, very, hard.

There is no need for anyone, particularly the person concerned, to know how you feel or what you are doing. There are many techniques that can be used to forgive people. You could write a letter and tear it up. You could visualise the other person sitting in a chair and tell that person how you feel, and imagine him or her telling the other side as well, to help you see things in a different light. If it's really difficult to forgive someone, try writing out 'I forgive you (person's name)', as many times as possible for seven days.

Forgiveness is not for the other person's benefit, it is for yours. You cannot succeed and get all that you want from life if you are wasting energy by being angry and hurt. Your focus is not on what you want, it is on the past. I have used some of these techniques and received a positive response from the parties involved, even though they didn't know what I was doing.

Exercise

Take one situation in your life, such as debts, lack of money, or job dissatisfaction. Write down what you gain from that situation.

_____

_____

_____

_____

Are you prepared to let it go?

_____

If you are not, then change your goal for the time being.

Try mentally forgiving yourself or another person for creating a problem you have. Mentally release this problem by saying 'I release the need for (job dissatisfaction/debts/ lack of love). I am willing to (enjoy work/be rich/loved)'.

List all the things you like about yourself. Dwell on your successes, and the aspects of your personality that you love.

CHAPTER 5

Overcoming obstacles

If there were no obstacles we would already have everything we want. Obstacles such as time, money, lack of training or fear, can all be overcome, but what if your obstacle is another person—possibly your husband—who handles all the money or spends too much? What if your children's needs are more important than your own, and they take every cent you earn. What can you do?

Other people

Our society encourages women to place themselves last. Their income, if they have one, is often gobbled up by bills and children's expenses. This situation builds resentment and a no-win condition can develop.

A client told me that during the time she was separated from her husband, she managed to pay all the bills and still save a few thousand dollars. Since the couple has been reconciled, they have no savings and always seem to be just scraping by. There is never money around when a bill falls due, although they still live in the same home and their combined income is greater. She cannot afford a night out, a holiday or even a facial.

It is very difficult for marriages to succeed while one partner feels valueless and is constantly suppressing anger. We cannot change anyone else, only ourselves. One partner, in an aggravating predicament such as this, can choose to react differently. The wife could insist on keeping a certain proportion of her wage for herself, or they could sit down together and decide on priorities, and allocate an allowance for both of them.

Recognise your own worth and put yourself first. This is not being selfish. The woman who allows herself to become a doormat, or plays the martyr, does not do her family a favour, nor is she the ideal role model for children.

Single women can make the same mistakes, only the players in the game are different. Too many women put men first, fitting in their own needs and desires after those of their man, the boss, or perhaps ageing parents.

You can put yourself first by paying yourself first. From your salary or whatever source of income you have, set aside an amount just for you, no matter how small to begin with. What you do with this money, whether you save it or spend it, is up to you. It is yours to enjoy.

The way most people manage money is to pay the mortgage, telephone and electricity bills, any accounts and so forth. Then if anything is left over they may spend it on themselves. There is nothing more frustrating than working all week and seeing everyone else benefit from your labour.

Recognition of your worth will come from others once you give it to yourself. Once you make allowances by paying yourself first, you will find that there is enough to pay the bills. It's the same as when you have a pay decrease, when one partner stops work, or you change jobs. Somehow you manage on the money available.

You will look after you

Men are encouraged to believe that they are responsible for their future and must work from an early age. Even in the 1980s, with attitudes to women so changed, some women are still waiting for a wealthy man to come along and rescue them. They regard work as something you do while you're waiting. A lot of my female clients still say 'well the only way I'll get anywhere is to find a wealthy man'. This is abdicating responsibility and for this reason many such women do not reach their full potential, because they do not commit themselves to a job or plan. In reality, women do not have this choice at all—it is only an illusion. No-one can be sure that there will always be someone to look after them.

Joan's husband died suddenly of a heart attack two years before he was due to retire. In her late fifties, Joan came from a generation where women were encouraged to be dependent. Joan and Roger had no children, no family and had lived mostly for each other.

When I first met Joan she couldn't write a cheque. A few months after her husband died her home was burnt down. Joan was lost. She had no experience dealing with insurance companies and as a consequence, lived in a hotel room for eighteen months while things were being sorted out.

After twelve months the insurance company ceased paying this rent and Joan had to dip into her savings. Meanwhile the building had been vandalised and there were complaints of mismanagement by the strata management company. The contents were not insured, so internal fittings were Joan's responsibility, and quotes for painting were outrageously high.

Although Joan's husband provided her with enough money, she was left without the necessary skills to handle problems and make decisions at a particularly painful period in her life.

It is far better to accept responsibility for your life now. Know about the family finances, know where the money goes, play an active role in decision-making. If you work, choose a career that you enjoy. Don't sit back and expect someone else to do for you what you will not do for yourself.

Competition can be win-win

Men tend to be natural competitors and women are not. This is probably a result of conditioning rather than genetics. Men can openly compete with each other and still be the best of friends, whereas many women find competition frightening and don't try.

In my family, my sister was the sporting champion, while I developed a reputation for being hopeless at anything athletic. I was the kid that the boys at tennis would try to avoid, saying, 'Oh, we don't really have to play with her!', so I stopped trying. Consequently as an adult, whenever competition walked in the door, I walked out. My excuse was that I didn't believe in competition, but the reality was that I was afraid of trying and failing.

There are many women just like me. We need to change our image from losers to winners and at the same time change the image of competition from a win-lose situation to a win-win situation. Competition enables you to develop strengths you might otherwise have neglected. It encourages you to improve your performance, to be the best you can be.

Women do not lose their femininity by being competitive. A tough, competitive, successful woman can still be caring, warm and feminine.

Discrimination—myths and realities

Very few women are discriminated against nowadays for housing or personal loans. Business loans are another matter, although in many instances I believe this is often the fault of the applicant.

To succeed in any business you need to be professional. Eighty per cent of all businesses fail within the first five years and many do not last that long, so banks and other lending institutions are justified in being selective. It is not good enough to decide that you want to open a shop and go along to the bank and ask for a loan. Yet, people do it every day. You need to know your market, product, and competition, as well as pricing, and some basic accounting. Men fail just as much as women in their lack of preparation.

Research, until you know your market and your product inside out. Make a business plan that encompasses marketing, costing, projected sales, overheads and cash flow. If you lack the expertise to make such a plan consult an accountant. It will be money well spent. Then, and only then, apply for a loan if necessary.

Fear does not keep you safe

As she placed a plastic shopping bag on my desk she said 'Will you take this money and do something with it please???' The bag contained $65 000 cash. It was late afternoon and the banks were closed. I refused to take responsibility for such a large amount overnight and asked her to return the next day. For two months she had been sleeping with this money under her pillow, too afraid to make a decision.

'My husband believes there is going to be another depression, so we thought we'd buy some gold bars and put them under the bed just in case', said another client.

'You know that little nest-egg that I told you about?', said Carol. 'Well it's $30 000 and it's wrapped in plastic in my kitchen freezer.' Over the three years that I'd known Carol she had often mentioned her little nest-egg, but I'd never taken much notice. When I asked why she had never put this money in a bank or invested it, she replied 'Every time I release money it never comes back. With my luck the bank will collapse. At least in the freezer I know it's safe'.

For years Carol had been wondering why her business was not growing, she had just enough to get by on, but never any more. If she gained a new client, she would lose an old one. 'Why?', she would ask, 'I've done everything I know, I'm good at what I do and I really believe I deserve to be prosperous.' The frozen money tells it all.

Money is just another form of energy that is neither good nor bad. Block that energy by placing it in a freezer, hiding it under the bed, or sleeping with it under a pillow and it will remain at a standstill. Money that is invested is energy in circulation. Money placed in a bank is lent to other people to buy houses and cars, to run businesses and so on. The flow is continuous.

There are many words representing fear and we can dress it up in a hundred disguises or call it by many names: anxiety, apprehension, concern, panic, worry. No matter how you express it, fear does not keep you safe. A fearful mentality manifests itself in financial difficulties, lack, crime, dishonesty, compulsive spending and health and relationship problems. Procrastination, wishful thinking or staying in a bad relationship, are all by-products of fear.

Some of the most common fears that I've come across are: fear of success . . . of failure . . . that there will not be enough . . . of making a fool of yourself . . . of making mistakes . . . of not being good enough . . . of being noticed . . . of loss of parental approval . . . of doing better than parents or partner . . . of change . . . of rejection . . . of discovery . . . of loss of prestige.

One client had a large sum of money in a non-interest bearing cheque account. I explained that she was losing $80 a day in interest, but she was so afraid of paying too much tax that she chose to pay no tax at all. This woman also had difficulty making decisions, so six months later the money was still in the cheque account. She could have earned $14 500 and tax would have taken no more than half the amount. Or, she could have given the interest to a tax deductible charity, and not had her personal tax affected.

Women in particular sabotage their progress, because many are not yet totally comfortable with success. Fear of doing better than our parents is a concern shared by both men and women. Some women feel consumed with guilt, for choosing to work instead of being a full-time mother. It all goes back to your upbringing and the roles and values that were instilled in you as a child. In some cultures a woman would feel guilty for not working.

Contrary to common opinion, fear is not a negative emotion. There are no negative emotions, only negative reactions. Feeling fearful is natural, but allowing fear to dominate your actions and decisions is limiting.

Gerald Jampolsky is a psychiatrist who works with terminally ill children. He is also the author of the book *Love is letting go of Fear*.[3] He believes that there are only two emotions: love and fear. Feelings such as anger, jealousy, envy and rejection, all stem from fear. He says that 'fear is really only a call for help'.

Living in the present moment

When you analyse fears, most of them are based on future events. What might happen if . . . ? The only moment we live in is the present one, and most fears never amount to anything.

At one time when money was in short supply, I asked Lionel Fifield for advice. Lionel is a leading public speaker on the subject of prosperity and someone I particularly admire. Instead of giving advice, he asked a few pertinent questions such as: 'Do you have a roof over your head? Do you have enough to eat? Is your health O.K.?' When

I answered yes to all the questions, he said 'Well what are you worried about?'. Once I looked at my situation from a different angle I realised things weren't so bad, and it was only a temporary problem. I promptly rang my creditors and advised that I couldn't make repayments on time and set about making the extra money.

Many women are unhappy in their marriages but will not leave because they fear the financial responsibility of bringing up children alone. One special friend was totally unhappy and confused. She said 'The past and the future have all merged, events have overtaken me and I've lost control'.

We never really lose control over our lives. We always have the choice of whether we will stay or leave a particular situation. We may choose to stay in that situation because we are not prepared to accept the consequences of change. It all comes back to 'choice'. When we get our emotions out of the way, we often find that we have more choices than we thought.

There are times when remaining in a bad relationship can be self-destructive. There are no guarantees of what tomorrow will bring. The only moment you can be sure of is this moment, right now.

In the early days when I was bringing up my children without support, I'd feel fearful and overwhelmed at times. Sometimes I just had to live one day at a time. When my son died in an accident, the only way I survived was to try to make it through one day. Sometimes even that was too much to cope with, so I would hang on to the minute. Life is not always easy. There have been times in my life when it all seemed just too much and I felt that there was no hope or no way out.

We cannot see around corners, and the future is often different to what we may think. Today, I am surrounded by so much love and although I don't yet have everything I want, I can give myself everything I need. I sometimes wonder what I would have missed if I had played it safe, and taken no chances.

Success does not separate us from other people; only fear does that. The best way to cope with fear is to learn to live in the present moment. You can never anticipate everything that could happen. However, if you are concerned about making a major decision or changing directions, it can help to have a contingency plan.

Contingency plans

I read once that a successful entrepreneur always had two or three contingency plans for any business venture he undertook. This particularly impressed me and it is a method I've used ever since. A contingency plan is not essential and it is not planning for disaster. It frees the mind to concentrate on the goal at hand, knowing that there are specific steps that can be taken if things do not go according to plan.

Gail's goal was to set up a marketing consultancy business. She had a number of plans for obtaining clients and enough money to live on for six-months. Her main concern was how to survive if it took longer than six months to generate enough business to support her, so she made three contingency plans. The first was to obtain part-time work if she did not look like meeting the six month deadline. Her second was to obtain a loan. Thirdly, she intended to seek out a partner to inject funds, if all else failed.

Having the security of three action plans behind her enabled Gail to concentrate on the important task of obtaining clients and building their businesses. She obtained part-time work for a short period, that was all. Gail said 'It gave me a tremendous sense of security knowing that I had a number of options to fall back on and that I didn't have to succeed at my first attempt'.

Feeling guilty can become a habit

Many women, more so older women, feel guilty spending money on themselves. In nearly every workshop that I run, a woman makes a remark like 'whenever I buy myself something I hide it away in the wardrobe, so my husband won't see it. A few months later when I drag it out and he asks if it's new I can truthfully say I've had it for months'. My own mother did the same thing or reduced the price of nearly all purchases for my father's benefit, yet my father would have given my mother anything. Until recently, I did the same thing and was not consciously aware of it.

For many of us this guilt is a habit and we are simply repeating a pattern established generations ago. How many men do you know who feel guilty about spending money on themselves? None that I know of. It has always been acceptable for a man to spend money any way he wants. This may have been the rule when men were the sole providers, but it serves no valid purpose today.

If you have some money to spare, spend it on yourself, then tell someone about it. If there is no-one at home, tell someone at work, or a neighbour. The idea is to become comfortable about spending money on yourself.

There are more serious aspects of feeling guilty. One man spends very little on himself but is always giving money to other people. His children are now adults but keep expecting Dad to come to their rescue. He admits to feeling guilty because his marriage broke up when the children were teenagers and he overcompensates by giving them whatever they want, often to their detriment. He sabotages himself constantly, and is always being used by other people.

There can be many reasons for feeling guilty. Marriage break-ups rate highly, so does leaving children, in order to work. But there are other reasons such as earning a higher income than your partner or friend, being promoted over someone else, being hopeless with money, not living up to other people's expectations. In the case of inherited wealth, some people feel guilty for enjoying someone else's money, or feel uncomfortable about having money they did not earn. Guilt can also stem from a religious upbringing.

Losing money doesn't accomplish anything except making you poorer. If guilt is a problem try sharing what you have with others. Giving benefits the giver and the receiver and is constructive rather than destructive. When we feel guilty we sabotage ourselves.

Forget willpower

Self-discipline is simply a matter of having a strong enough desire. Find one reason for achieving your goal and concentrate on that.

People who have been overweight for years and then had a health scare, suddenly find it easy to lose weight. Another young man I heard of was hopeless at school, receiving marks of less than ten out of a hundred for most subjects even though his family tried everything to get him to study. When he attended Technical College to study boat building, he came top of the class.

Katy never had the discipline to save on a regular basis, and constantly overspent on her credit cards. After one trip, eating and drinking her way through Europe, she decided to do something about it. She attended one of my courses, and realised that she perpetuated the problem by constantly moaning on the phone, to her girlfriend, about how poor she was.

She started buying herself flowers every week, stopped talking about her problems, and we rearranged her debts so that she could save each week. Within six months the change was incredible. She had achieved all of her goals, one of which was to spend six weeks in France studying French, and is now thinking of buying a farmhouse there.

'Once, I would never have aimed so high because it seemed too far out of reach. I'd tried saving before and had never had any success. Now it doesn't seem hard at all, and I should have my holiday home within a year.'

Forget willpower—it doesn't work. Often it only reinforces feelings of failure. Find one good reason to achieve your goal and the discipline will follow.

Study in your spare time

Lack of knowledge can be a major stumbling block, particularly if work or family pressures prevent you from attending the appropriate course. Time spent travelling to and from work can be utilised to read and study. If you drive, listen to audio cassette programs. There are cassettes available on most subjects. Study by correspondence, or, if you don't want to put in the effort to study for years, research if there are other ways to gain the experience, or achieve your goal without actually attending college. Don't be deterred by a belief that you have to have a degree, or have a certain level of intelligence. Sometimes there is another way.

While my children were little I studied business letter writing, accountancy, economics, business communication and art, all by correspondence and at no cost. Although I didn't finish many of these courses, I gained a wealth of knowledge that is invaluable today.

Do you really need money?

Ah, the things we would do, if only we had the money! Well, maybe we don't need it.

Very few entrepreneurs have large sums of money when they first start out. Lack of money gives you the opportunity to be creative, to come up with new ideas, and new ways to do things. Rather than take out a hefty loan to start a business, consider starting on a smaller scale. Businesses run from home have smaller overheads and significant tax benefits. The less pressure you place upon yourself when starting out, the more likely you are to succeed.

One man I worked with wanted an outdoor garden setting, but lacked the funds to buy one. He bought plastic tubing from a plumbing supplier and experimented with it. He made a fantastic garden setting at a fraction of the cost, and came up with a new business in the process.

A former business partner of mine lost a lot of money when his first business went into liquidation. He was left with substantial debts. At the same time an investment that he had contributed to for many years collapsed. As a temporary measure, he took a job selling kitchens and discovered a talent for design he didn't know he possessed. Within months he became the company's top salesperson.

He persuaded the management to allow him to open a franchise showroom. As this was an experiment, there was no fee involved and the company arranged for the leasing of the kitchens and all equipment needed. Bill borrowed just a few thousand to tide him over. Within six months he had a team of seven sales people, and the highest sales of all branches. During that first six months he took a substantial wage, fitted out the office, and there was still money left over, as the business began making profits from the first month.

Admittedly this man was good at marketing, but I believe his success came not from his management ability, but from his belief in himself. At an early age he excelled at sport. While in his teens he was offered a contract to play soccer for England and for a few years he represented Australia in the World Cup series. There are many people who have excelled at sport who go on to be successful in business. It's because they have become comfortable with success at an early age, and they have learnt to focus on what they want.

My first business was started with absolutely no capital at all. Clients have bought homes without an initial deposit, while others have bought investment property without any capital.

At twenty-eight, Sue decided it was time she started doing something sensible with her money. She earned a good income but up to now had spent most of it on clothes and overseas trips. She had the earning capacity to repay a large loan, so we decided that an investment property was the best way for her to start, as she did not have the patience to save for years. She freely admitted she was one of those people who wanted to see results quickly, or she would lose interest.

We calculated that it would take twelve months at least for her to save a deposit, and that was living very stringently. The rent she would receive from the property would go towards a large proportion of the loan payment. Within two months she rang back to say a friend had the money for a deposit, but not the capacity to borrow the amount required, so they joined forces.

There are many ways and countless opportunities and we do get more than one chance. Don't block them by believing that you have to have an exact amount of money, or achieve a goal in a specific way. Concentrate on what you want, not on how to get it.

Is there ever enough time?

Time is a major problem for many people. It can also be an excellent excuse. Time management techniques can be learned by anyone. They say if you want something done, give it to a busy person. Successful people are busy, because they constantly attract opportunities to them. We all have exactly the same amount of time available. When you manage time efficiently you get more done in less time, and you feel good about yourself.

I had been conditioned to think that running a business and a home was a full-time job. But there was more I wanted to do, so I began running prosperity workshops in the evening and writing this book in my spare time. A few months ago, I had a baby as well.

It has not all been smooth sailing, there are hiccups, but on the whole it works well. Some jobs like house-cleaning I've given away altogether and someone does that for me. Simple administration jobs I've delegated to an assistant, but I could not do this if I was not organised. Being a full-time mother is important to me, as are my clients and my work, so I set priorities and I have learnt to be flexible. Some days everything does go according to plan; other days I have to let go of my expectation and do what I can.

What would you do if you had more time? Write, study, start a business, travel, renovate a home? We all think we would do more, but chances are you wouldn't. Time or money are not the real reasons you don't do what you want. When the desire is strong enough, you will find both the time and the money.

How much of your time is taken up doing things that you don't want to do, all because you find it difficult to say no? If you cannot refuse, do an assertiveness training course and learn how.

Loving yourself means that *your* time is valuable too. Children do not become independent or responsible by always having their own personal taxi. Attitudes have changed and women are no longer expected to be door-mats. A family is a unit and each member benefits more by contributing to it. In my family, my children were able to choose which household jobs they wanted to do. They then had to commit themselves to doing those jobs by a certain day and time each week. They also chose beforehand which extra jobs they would do if they did not fulfil this commitment. It works.

Being organised takes commitment, but once you've

mastered it, you will wonder why you didn't do it sooner. A habit is developed by starting. Make an announcement to family and friends. Make it difficult for yourself to give up easily. Allow no exceptions and stick with your new resolution. Act upon it at every opportunity.

If you cannot manage alone, get help. No-one expects you to be superwoman, except yourself. Stop saying 'I must get organised one day'. Start now.

Security comes from within

On the whole, security is a high priority for most women. Achieving goals doesn't mean you have to take risks, especially when it comes to investments. Money can be invested in secure investments and as long as tax and inflation are taken into account when planning, your money should do the work for you.

Take my friend with the $30 000 in her kitchen freezer. If this money had been invested for three years at 14 per cent and interest rates were at that level over that period, it would have grown to $44 000. I have seen people lose thousands each year because they didn't know where to go for advice, so they opted for security by placing money in a low interest savings account.

One client had $25 000 in an account that was paying 3.75 per cent. By simply transferring this over to another account within the same bank, she could have made another $1 800 a year. Over five years that adds up to $9 000. Unfortunately, financial institutions exploit people like this. If someone is benefiting from your money, then it may as well be you.

Investments, or money in the bank can make you feel secure, but the only real security comes from within. By developing confidence in your own abilities, you will be able to adapt to changing circumstances and therefore find real peace of mind.

Exercise

What obstacles do you relate to?

_____

_____

_____

How can you overcome them?

_____

_____

CHAPTER 6

The powers of your mind

Once, not that long ago, people who believed in mind powers or positive thinking were considered a bit odd. When Dr Norman Vincent Peale first wrote *The Power of Positive Thinking* he was nearly forced to give up his ministry. Nowadays, because of the stresses of modern living, more and more people are looking at new ways to cope.

Everyday living in cities is stressful. Commuting to work, the noise and fumes of traffic, unemployment and playing office politics are all stress-producing situations. Women particularly have more financial pressures than ever before, often combining a career and family. Standards of living and expectations are higher. Single women are expected to own their own home, although salaries for women are still less than those of their male counterparts.

As increasing numbers want more from life than just getting by, they tend to open up to new opportunities— new ways to do things. Instead of becoming tense and consciously striving to achieve goals you can learn to relax and allow your mind to create your reality—the way you want it to be. By understanding how the mind works you gain the freedom to choose rather than allowing yourself to be dictated to by circumstances.

The invention of computers, electronic communication systems and other devices led scientists to explore how the human mind functions. They discovered that parts of the human mind operate automatically, much like an electronic computer. Present it with a success goal and it will achieve success. Present it with a failure goal and it will achieve failure. There are three levels to the human mind: the conscious, the subconscious and the intuitive mind.

The conscious mind

We operate in the state of consciousness most of our waking time. The conscious mind makes decisions, plans, rationalises and performs all the everyday tasks. It is not the conscious mind that runs your life . . . .it is the subconscious.

The subconcious mind

It has been said that the subconscious is not really a mind at all. It is an impersonal mechanism. It does not judge, or make decisions, it simply sets out to fulfil any goals programmed into it. Therein lies your personal freedom.

The subconscious is also a storehouse. Everything that has ever happened to you, everything that you have ever read or seen is filed away in the memory banks. These memory banks contain hundreds of beliefs on a whole range of subjects. You may have a program that you are friendly or shy; good with money or hopeless with money; lovable or unlovable; clever or stupid. These beliefs are not necessarily right or wrong—they just are.

The subconscious simply gives back whatever has been programmed into it. Just like a computer, programs can be changed. Gaining control and choosing the programs to be held in your subconscious is the way to achieve financial freedom, or anything else that you want from life. Intelligence, background, education, sex or age play no role here. Re-program your mental computer and you will change your life.

Most of our beliefs are picked up from our parents, who probably picked them up from their parents, and so patterns of thinking are established. The validity of these beliefs is rarely questioned. In his book, *The Double Win*[4], Denis Waitley tells a story of a woman who always cut off both ends of the ham when she put it into the baking dish. When her husband asked why, she said she didn't know why, but she knew that was the way it was done because her mother had always done it that way. He then asked her mother, and got a similar reply. So he asked the grandmother. She replied that she always cut the ends off the ham because the baking dish was too small and it wouldn't fit otherwise.

I was fortunate to have a mother who told me I was clever. At school I was always average, at I.Q tests I was always average, I even failed an entrance exam to work behind the counter at Woolworths. None of this mattered, because my subconscious belief was that I was clever, my mother had always told me so—and I became what I believed.

Most people work on solving problems at a conscious level. Using the intellect, or conscious mind, we rationalise what we feel and try to find solutions. It is an exhausting and ineffective method.

This is why positive thinking alone does not work. Positive thinking works at a conscious level. It is a way of constantly rising above one's problems, never dealing with the real issues or changing subconscious beliefs. If your subconscious belief is not in agreement with your conscious belief, you will get what you believe at the subconscious level. This may not necessarily be what you want.

The simplest way to check what your deep-seated beliefs are is to look at your life. What does it tell you? Do you have the money you want, the lifestyle, relationship, job? If you answer 'no' to any of these questions then you may need to discover what subconscious belief is holding you back and replace it with the belief of your choice. People say 'but I do believe I should have more money', and that's usually true, but only on a conscious level. Underneath that there are other messages. The outer reflection of your life does not lie.

Uncovering subconscious beliefs may not be as easy as it sounds, because we build up defences over a long period of time. A newborn child has no sense of self; his sense of self-worth is built up gradually and his parents' verbal and non-verbal messages slowly formulate his self-image. If a parent describes a child as bad or stupid, then that child believes it. Imagine this same message repeated over a number of years. A child whose parents rarely play with him or spend no time with him, will conclude that his parents don't like him and so he will reject himself.

By the time the child is old enough to start school he has heard many messages like 'I can hardly wait till he goes to school'; 'Why aren't you as clever as your sister?'; 'Don't trust him to bring anything home, he has a terrible memory'. Single messages, or isolated moments of anger do not usually harm a child. It is the consistent messages that may be uttered unintentionally that program the subconscious.

To very young children parents are perfect and can do no wrong, so they accept the messages they hear without question and they may decide that they are pretty stupid or worthless. By age five, a child has built up a fairly complete picture of who he is. Prior to age five very few of us have much recall, so it is only natural that we are not consciously aware of the messages that we picked up. Parents are not totally responsible, but they play the most important role.

There are people who had a less than perfect childhood and have done well, but at what cost? There are workaholics, who may be successful in their careers, but have little success in personal relationships. They live behind a facade of success, and being too busy is a good excuse not to have to face difficult issues in their personal life. This is very much a male trait. I have met so many outwardly successful people, who have said to me that they feel like frauds. We cannot change our childhood, but we can change our future by re-programming these beliefs and by learning to use intuition.

The intuitive mind

We all possess intuition and some are more practised at using it than others. The intuitive mind is the creative genius within us. It functions twenty-four hours a day. Like the subconscious, it never sleeps; it has access to the sub-conscious, but unlike it, the intuitive mind can assess all the facts and return the perfect solution to any problem.

The intuitive mind can communicate with other minds and has access to universal knowledge. Clairvoyants, psychics, people who communicate through E.S.P., all have highly-developed intuitive minds, as do many successful business people. Children between the ages of two to four test out at 96 per cent genius level for creativity, but by age seven they only test out at 4 per cent.

The intuitive mind has many names. Some call it the higher self, the superconscious, the spirit, soul, or just plain intuition. Whatever you call it, it can be your greatest ally.

Everyone can develop their intuitive powers. We communicate with this mind through relaxation. The solutions to every problem are within you. Simply ask your higher self for guidance, during a relaxed state. Again, forget the 'how to' in achieving your goal. That is the role of the conscious mind. Simply focus on what you want, by using your intuitive mind. The means will take care of itself.

Often, the answer will come when you least expect it; sometimes in a dream, or you will awake during the night; or while doing something entirely different, a flash of inspiration will come. Don't ignore it when it does. We often ask for answers, then forget to listen. Your intuition cannot get through if you are constantly busy, surrounded by people and your mind is always chattering. A regular quiet time is essential.

Years ago I worked as a bookkeeper and often the monthly accounts would not reconcile when I tried to balance the ledgers. Sometimes I would work overtime checking and re-checking figures, only to have the answer pop into my head while I was having a shower at home.

If you are having a problem with money, whether it is how to make more or what to do with the money you have, ask your intuitive mind for guidance and help. Keep asking until you have an answer. When the time is right, the right people, ideas, course or book will emerge to provide the solution if you are receptive to it.

Haven't you ever felt you should slow down when driving, only to discover that there is a highway patrol over the next hill? It's all intuition.

Left brain/right brain activities

We can access the intuitive mind and re-program the subconscious through the conscious mind. The conscious mind has two distinct control centres. The left brain controls memory, speech, logic, mathematics, rational thinking. The left brain thinks in words. The right brain is the creative centre. It accesses the intuitive mind through pictures. The right brain is the centre of imagination, ideas, emotions and humour, as well as being the co-ordinating force for the physical body and controller of rhythm and movement.

We live in a predominantly left brain society and individuals who are predominantly right brain users have sometimes been out of place in the community. Thomas Edison, the greatest inventor of all time, was told as a child that he was too stupid to learn. Yet he used his intuitive mind to produce some of his most famous inventions. Beethoven, acknowledged as one of the world's greatest composers, was considered a failure by his music teacher. Albert Einstein did not talk until he was three.

Unfortunately, our education system favours left brain thinkers. Children who are predominantly right brain thinkers are put down often as being slow, stupid or troublesome. This creates a program in their subconscious and these children grow to adulthood believing they are not as good as their peers. No wonder things always go wrong for them.

Relationships, jobs, income and health all reflect our subconscious beliefs. People who never have any money, hate their jobs and have health problems are no worse than their opposites. They just have a different program. Statistics show that children of divorced parents have a higher rate of divorce; children who are brought up by foster parents have a higher incidence of having their own children fostered. It has nothing to do with genetics, or bad blood, as they used to say many years ago. These people are not failures, they have simply adopted their parents' pattern of thinking.

Change your beliefs at a subconscious level and the world around you changes and people change. Relationships that have previously been difficult become harmonious, or the people concerned drift out of your life. Money flows through many channels. A new job may come along, or the present one might improve.

Don't worry about or focus on the mistakes you make. Success is achieved by forgetting mistakes and remembering the successes. You cannot succeed if you never fail. Persistence is what separates the 'haves' from the 'have nots'. You have all the power you ever need already, within your own mind.

In recent years, research has shown that the development of either brain is a result of learning and mental exercise. In order to re-program the subconscious using the left brain, we use affirmations. We re-program the subconscious using the right brain by means of visualisation techniques. When both brains work in harmony, then you will achieve your goal much more easily and effortlessly.

Minds communicate

We know that some people communicate telepathically, but did you know that a small number of people with a common goal can change the world?

Ken Keyes Jr. wrote the book *The Hundredth Monkey*[5] in a bid to save the world from nuclear devastation. In this book he tells the story of the Japanese monkey living in the wild on the island of Koshima.

Scientists had been feeding the monkeys sweet potatoes, by dropping them in the sand. An eighteen-month-old female monkey started to wash the potatoes in a nearby stream. She taught this new skill to her mother and playmates. Over a six year period all the young monkeys on the island learned to wash their sweet potatoes before eating, but some of the adults still continued to eat them covered in sand.

One day a change occurred. The exact number of monkeys washing their sweet potatoes is unknown, but as one extra monkey joined in, presumably the hundredth monkey as the title suggests, EVERYONE in the tribe began washing the sweet potatoes before eating them.

Not only were all the monkeys on Koshima washing their sweet potatoes, but at the same time, colonies of monkeys on neighbouring islands did so as well. Ken Keyes

Jr. believes that it was the added energy of that hundredth monkey that created the breakthrough. We can use this same energy by combining our thoughts to create a better, safer world.

Look at the world around you. We constantly hear of world debts, budget deficits, personal debt. The share-market crash of 1987 received more publicity than any good financial news that I can remember. The economy is governed by supply and demand . . . and emotions.

If more individuals changed their subconscious expec-tancy from fear and lack, to abundance and prosperity, this feeling of optimism and well-being would influence those around them. Feelings of optimism are just as contagious as feelings of pessimism. As the numbers grow, a shift in the consciousness of nations could occur, as happened with the monkeys.

Instead of a false prosperity created by credit, there could be abundance for everyone. This may be an idealistic dream, but what is the alternative? Join with mass consciousness in the false belief that there is not enough to go around? Our unemployment figures confirm that this is what a lot of people believe. We do have a say about the world we live in, we can choose to be responsible for our own prosperity and we can influence others positively. Your thoughts, joined with mine and thousands of others, can bring about change. ONE PERSON DOES MAKE A DIFFERENCE.

Synergy

As an individual you have certain talents and when you combine these talents with other like-minded individuals, you leave mediocrity behind and become achievers of excellence. The synergy principle is that 'the whole is greater than the sum of its parts'. Synergy principles are often used in team sports. John Bertrand, who skippered the Australia II to victory in the 1983 America's Cup said 'It was a team effort, a team win'[6]. The team involved not just the crew, but those behind the scenes as well.

Synergy occurs when goals are in alignment and everyone is working for the same thing. When you are part of the decision-making process, your opinion counts, therefore your interest is likely to be greater. Japanese management has used this method for many years and Japan is now overtaking America as the world's leading nation.

In my prosperity workshops participants work in pairs to support each other in achieving goals by affirming and visualising for each other. While you may have difficulty changing an old belief, or get stuck in trying to find a solution, another person often has no trouble seeing you as having achieved your goal. This added energy sometimes makes a difference. Not everyone succeeds, for varying reasons, but the successes outweigh the failures.

Make a supporting cast

Choose someone to work with you, someone who believes you can achieve your goal, to make up a supporting cast. It could consist of your parents, partner, children, friends, family, boss, co-workers, clients, accountant, teachers or financial advisers. It may be a group or just one person.

As a financial adviser, my goal is to help my clients to prosper, which is usually their goal too. By working together, we achieve the double win. If I do the best thing by my clients and put their best interests first, before commissions or sales figures, then ultimately I win by having satisfied clients. Satisfied clients refer their friends to me and it is the most cost-effective way of increasing business. My role is to help clients achieve their dreams in the most efficient way, without enforcing my ideas or values. Whether you are self-employed or employed, synergy can be utilised so that everyone wins.

Join with your employer to make the business more profitable. Self-employed people can work with their customers, no matter what business they are in. At home, join together as a family, to achieve certain goals. Parents are not always solely responsible for providing everything for the family, so have projects in which every member plays a role. We gain the most by working together.

CHAPTER 7

The turning point

There are no right ways or wrong ways to reshape your life, just different ways. Just as there is no level of prosperity that is right or wrong, the choice is purely individual. Most people who read this book though, would probably want more than they presently have, be it money or lifestyle. If you want your life to be different, try the methods outlined in this chapter for thirty consecutive days. If they do not work, all you have lost is some time. If they do work for you, then you will have discovered not only the path to financial freedom, but a way to change your entire life.

When you change your thoughts, you change your world. What you thought yesterday, has created your world today; what you think today, creates your world for tomorrow. So choose the thoughts that will shape your life the way you want it to be, rather than letting your mind worry, or wander aimlessly. By all means make practical plans to achieve goals, but learn to attract opportunities to you as well. Thoughts and words can attract or repel opportunities.

Just about everything in this universe is a form of energy. There are two forms of energy, materialised and unmaterialised. Materialised energy is anything tangible such as furniture, cars, houses, cash. Unmaterialised energy is something you cannot see, such as thoughts and words. You can learn to use this energy to your advantage. If you find it hard to accept that thoughts are energy, just think for a moment about a time when you felt exhausted and something unexpected and exciting happened. Suddenly you experienced a burst of energy. Or think how exhausted you felt after being with a negative person all day. I've always noticed whenever we have a lot of people together in a workshop, how the heat builds up in the room. Heat is energy.

To bring about positive changes in our lives, we need to harness and use our energy efficiently. We can do this by using our thoughts and words as affirmations.

Affirmations

Affirmations are positive statements, repeated over and over. They are simply another form of self-talk, but this time you are programming your subconscious with thoughts of what you want, rather than fear and worry.

If you have had years of negative reinforcement, then it takes time to re-program the subconscious with a new belief. An affirmation repeated several times a day for eight days is nearly memorised. But nearly memorised is not good enough to change your life. If you read this book only once and do no more, you will have forgotten practically all of it within thirty days. Repetition pays off.

When I want to change a belief, or situation in my life, I repeat an affirmation every time I think of it, for thirty days. For me that length of time seems to be all I need. I have also found that looking at myself in the mirror while affirming something helps, so whenever I put on makeup, brush my hair, or clean my teeth, I usually say something positive to myself.

Another method is to write down your affirmation. This method is helpful if you can't solve a problem, or if you retain knowledge better if you see it written down.

Affirmation is not wishful thinking. It is a method of accessing the subconscious mind by using the left brain. An affirmation is a positive statement of fact, not hope, because once the subconscious accepts it, and the subconscious does not judge or rationalise, it is merely a matter of time before it becomes a reality. You may not feel positive at first, while your are re-programming your mental computer, but feeling doubtful will not stop the process from working. Your actions are what counts.

Some people use the excuse 'I don't have time' but there are many opportunities during the day for affirmations which don't interfere with your normal routine. There is time while you are in the shower, driving to work, doing exercises, housework, or anything repetitive. If you can't find the time, then you don't really want to change yet.

Excuses are only another form of resistance. If someone said to you 'You can have anything you want but you will have to spend fifteen minutes a day working for it' would you really say 'I don't have time'?

Florence Scovel Shinn wrote about using affirmations back in 1925, in her book *The Game of Life*[7], so the idea is not new. She says when you can 'wish without worrying', every desire will be instantly fulfilled. My desire to make a career change is a perfect illustration of how quickly affirmations can make things happen.

At that time I was working as office manager for an investment company. I enjoyed working with investments but was bored with administration work, and hated office politics. I knew precisely what I wanted in a new position, but not the exact job that would fulfil my requirements. I also knew I wanted to be self employed but lacked sufficient money to start a business of the type I wanted. One day, feeling thoroughly fed up with looking and waiting, I decided 'enough was enough'. There was a perfect job for me and it would come to me without any more effort on my part. All the way to work I affirmed 'I have a perfect job in a perfect way and it will be offered to me today'. I said this for about fifteen minutes non-stop. At 8.30 am I arrived at the office and set about my duties and thought no more about it.

At 10 am I received a phone call from a man I knew

only slightly. He asked if I was happy in my present position and suggested that I come to see him. This interview led to a position that filled my criteria exactly . . . except that it was not my own business.

Six months later the opportunity arose to continue this work on a franchise basis; this enabled me to continue doing the work that I loved but gave me the independence of running my own business. Not only did I have an established business that had had the benefit of a large publicity campaign, but I also was given additional items such as stationery and promotional material at no cost. Subsequently I only needed a small amount of capital.

I later learned that the man responsible for my good fortune had been trying to contact me for six months, only I was never available. The opportunity had been there for me all the time. Only when I shifted my focus from the problems and frustrations I experienced, and focused on the position I wanted, using affirmations, did the opportunity present itself. I've experienced this so many times that I know it is not just coincidence.

How many opportunities are you missing by misdirecting your energy?

Quite often once a person has affirmed and been successful, she immediately stops. Success of this type can be shortlived. The belief must be sufficiently impressed on the subconscious mind for it to have lasting effects. It very much depends upon the condition you are trying to change. If you are affirming for a new job and you get one, there seems little point to continue, but if you often have problems at work, then you may wish to change your affirmation to include being happy in this new job. If you are trying to change a situation that has been a part of your life for a long time, then continue with your affirmation for the full thirty days. If you decide to rephrase your affirmation, then say the new one for thirty days.

At other times you may start affirming and everything goes wrong, with conditions seeming worse than they originally were. This is merely resistance coming to the surface. It is not uncommon for people affirming for prosperity to lose a wallet or large sum of money. Have you ever been on your way to a job interview and lost your résumé? It is all resistance. When these things happen, it is wise to rephrase your affirmation.

For instance you may have been affirming 'I am wealthy'. Try saying 'I allow myself to be wealthy', or, 'I deserve to be wealthy'. Once you feel comfortable with this new phrase, revert back to the original one. If an affirmation brings no results, try another. Experiment until you find the method that works for you.

An associate was trying to build up her client base by saying 'success is coming', but not a lot happened. I commented that this affirmation was putting success off until some future date; she was not focusing on the present. She changed her affirmation to 'I'm successful now', and obtained a new client that day.

Be careful what you ask for as you will probably get it. My friend Kristine wanted a man. Not just any man, there were certain attributes that this man had to have, and he had to love her son. She found him . . . he fitted the bill exactly, only there was no attraction on her side. She often said 'I got exactly what I asked for, but I forgot to say that I would love him too, I've tried and tried to love him, he's everything I ever wanted . . . but there's nothing there'.

Be specific as to what you want. In Kristine's case she would have had better results with 'I love and am loved by my perfect partner'. If she wanted to be married to him then this should have been added as well.

Affirmations must be positive. They must be in the present tense. They can be said anytime, though it will probably help you develop the habit by saying them at a set time each day to begin with. Personalise an affirmation so that you feel comfortable with it. At first you may find it easier to select one from the list below, but add to it to suit your particular goal:

I am paid to enjoy myself
I approve of myself
I always have lots of money
It is fun to be wealthy
I forgive myself for getting into debt
I forgive myself for wasting money
It's O.K. for me to be wealthy
I deserve to prosper
Prosperity zooms to me now
All my needs are met now
I am successful in everything I undertake
Everyday is a wonderful day, I attract opportunities to
    me
I am always in the right place at the right time
Wonderful opportunities flow to me now
I love myself
I allow myself to prosper
I feel comfortable being rich
I am immune to hurt and resentment
I enjoy being me

Affirm for what you want, NOT HOW TO GET IT. If you want a red sports car affirm 'I have a red sports car', not 'I have a loan to buy the car'. You may win the car, be given one, anything can happen. When you have a specific goal use a specific affirmation. When life is running smoothly you may prefer to use an all-encompassing affirmation to keep you on track, such as:

I love and approve of myself. I deserve the best of everything. My income is constantly increasing, I prosper in everything I do, and everyone around me prospers. I give thanks that all my needs are met. I am always surrounded by love. I am supported in everything I do. What I receive I lovingly share. My life is perfect right now.

Goals can be added in, others taken out, and remember to personalise any affirmation. The important message is loving and approving of yourself. From that everything else comes. Affirm each morning before you shower or dress, and again each night, and every time during the day that you think of it.

Ensure that your actions do not contradict the words of your affirmations. If you have a lot of debts and you mentally rehearse what to say to your creditors for making a late payment, then you would defeat an affirmation like 'I always have lots of money'.

Actions and affirmations must be in alignment. The debts cannot be ignored, so contact creditors and explain your circumstances. Use an affirmation such as 'I forgive myself for getting into debt, I now allow myself to prosper'. Feeling fearful does not count as long as you don't let it influence your actions, and you do not give it any more power by dwelling on it.

Focus on what you want and affirm daily. Author Louise Hay[2] suggests saying 'I approve of myself' hundreds of times a day. Many people with money problems have never had any real approval. We may have love, but love is not necessarily approval. How often can you recall anyone telling you that they approve of you? Don't wait for it to come from outside, you can give it yourself.

When my baby Laura was born, I expected everything to be smooth sailing, and to have a placid happy baby. Unfortunately it didn't work that way—babies have individual personalities and needs. Laura is a fairly demanding child, so I have tried affirming to her particularly when she is upset. Saying 'I approve of you' does seem to make a difference, particularly when she is teething. Affirmations and massage seem to be more effective than painkillers, and it is certainly preferable to walking the floor.

Affirmations work, but if you feel you need to take extra steps then do. Affirmations can provide the impetus to get started. Another client had always been reasonably successful but never felt it, because although her life was good, it was not the life that she wanted.

She had had success with affirmations previously and decided to keep affirming for the life that she wanted until she got it. She also meditated and visualised each day. This caused a lot of buried hurts and anger to rise to the surface. Her dreams were particularly informative. She realised that her self-image was of someone who always came last and no amount of success in the business world altered that.

She was able to relate this back to her childhood failure to achieve anything at sport. To many people this wouldn't matter, but she came from a family that excelled at sport and she was always a loser. She described it as 'always being on the outside looking in', and that was what her personal life reflected. She had always had a secret ambition to run a marathon. The affirmations provided her with the motivation to do it. She said 'This is something I am not doing for anyone else but myself. No amount of visualising will change my self-image until I do something physical'.

Sometimes an affirmation will present an opportunity to you, as in the case of my job offer. At other times, it will bring an old thought pattern to the surface so that you can change the belief. Or, it may bring a particular person into your life who will assist you. There are many possibilities, so do not close doors by stipulating how or where something will occur. The end result is what is important.

Affirmations access the intuitive mind through the left brain and when you use both the left and right brain, the results come effortlessly. We use the right brain by visualising our life the way we want it to be.

Start visualising

John Bertrand skippered the *Australia II* to victory in the 1983 America's Cup. In his book[8], he says:

' . . . the feeling that we had all been there before would have to be a part of our psychological makeup. Laurie knew all about this, and produced a plan for the mental visualisation of victory in Newport. Remember, you cannot go anywhere, if you have not first imagined yourself there. People achieve that which they have imagined themselves achieving over and over in their own minds. That which you have never even dreamed of is that which you will never attain.

. . . Every night before I went to sleep, I shut myself away and lived in my own mind the feeling of being in front, in the quiet, in the midst of the tension. And as I dreamed my separate dreams, it became easier. The power of the mind is enormous and together we sensed ourselves making it happen. Sometimes I would finish my fifteen-minute long session with my heart pounding and my pulse racing and the others said the same thing.'

He also said that they imagined the cries of the American team from behind, to expand their comfort zone. Visualisation is more than just making mental pictures, it's an all-encompassing image that includes sounds, smells and emotions. The more real it is to you the more likely it will become reality.

Affirmations alone work. Visualisation alone works. Together they become an incredibly powerful force.

Alpha brainwaves

By measuring brainwaves with an electro-encephalograph machine, scientists have discovered that the mind emits waves or impulses at four different levels. These levels are Beta, Alpha, Theta and Delta. Beta is our normal conscious level, in which state we think, play, feel emotions and try to work out problems. As we relax, our brainwaves slow from a normal Beta level of 14–26 cycles per second to an Alpha state which is 8–13 cycles per second. It is a state of deep relaxation, passiveness, almost like going into automatic.

Although we generally achieve an alpha state through

meditation or relaxation there can be times when doing something repetitive, such as driving a car, or typing, will trigger this state. Day-dreaming is usually done while at an Alpha level.

At the Theta level the brain slows to 4–7 cycles per second, which is usual for when we are asleep and the Delta level of ½–3½ cycles per second is usually an unconscious state.

It is the Alpha state that concerns us here. It is not hypnosis, as you are aware and in control at all times and you can learn to go into your Alpha level whenever you wish. It is the level at which very young children operate when they do their greatest amount of learning. Slowing your mind through relaxation or meditation is the easiest way to reach the Alpha level. You then access your intuitive mind, which has the answer to all that concerns you. Don't be put off by the word meditation. There are many different forms and you don't have to sit cross-legged and chant 'OM' to meditate. The objective is to slow the brainwaves to 8–13 cycles per second, using any method you find suitable.

When you are in this relaxed state you can visualise your day the way you want it to be. If you have a problem with another person, then mentally rehearse your conversation with him or her making sure the images this time are the ones you want. Resist the temptation to replay unhappy events, which only magnifies the problem by putting more energy into it.

See yourself travelling to work and arriving calm and relaxed; imagine yourself surrounded by a glass shield so that stress and tension cannot enter. There are any number of mental images that you can create to make life better. At the end of the day replay the day's events. If things did not go the way you hoped, replay them the way you want them to be. This is programming your mind positively for the next time that same situation occurs.

Try this method next time you want a parking spot.

Before starting your journey sit quietly and see yourself driving straight up to the perfect parking spot—no going around the block a few times—it is just as easy to get it first time. My friend Carolyn always left her car at the wharf and caught a ferry into the city, because she believed it was too difficult to park, until she tried this method. Now she drives every time and always finds a parking spot easily. Try it and see!

If you have difficulty creating mental pictures, don't worry. We assimilate and interpret information through many senses. Often one of these senses is more predominant than the others. Many creative people are highly visual; an interior decorator or artist can mentally see the image down to the smallest detail. A musician or composer may not be able to see a picture, but he can hear every sound and identify individual instruments in an orchestra. An actress can often feel a role, by identifying with the emotions of her character. It does not matter which senses come into play when meditating. Like John Bertrand, you will eventually be able to 'smell, taste and touch that feeling of total self-control'[9].

At one time I was a bookkeeper, a single parent with two children and a very average income. I've always been able to see myself as a public speaker, an author and running my own business. I first saw this image thirteen years ago when it seemed virtually impossible to achieve. It is an image that popped into my mind of its own accord, and opportunities have continued to present themselves to bring this vision to fruition. When you feel drawn to a particular job or place, it is often your intuition guiding you.

A girl I know used the visualiation method successfully. She had a good job, and was paying off her own unit. Her salary only covered her lifestyle as it was then and did not allow for overseas trips or investments. Her goal was to double her salary and she knew there were no opportunities to do this in her current position.

So she visualised. Within weeks an opportunity arose for her to go into a business requiring only a few thousand dollars capital. She applied, against a great deal of competition and was quite prepared to let this opportunity pass if it was not right for her. She was chosen from fifty other people.

Within three years she more than doubled her salary, bought two investment units that have since doubled in value. Most importantly, she is living the life that she always desired and she works less hours.

It is perfectly acceptable to create the image you want, but allow your mind time just to be still. Too often we pray and ask for solutions, yet never stop to listen. When in an Alpha state we access our intuition, so we should allow it to guide us. No matter how unrealistic a goal may appear now, if you can see it in your mind as being real, without forcing, then you can dismiss it from your consciousness, knowing that it will be achieved in time.

Visualising is not manipulation. You constantly make mental images whether you realise it or not. Haven't you ever replayed an argument, or a mistake you make at work? This only impresses the subconscious with images that you don't want. If you try to force an image you will not remain in an Alpha state. You will soon become tense and you will not get what you want.

Visualise what you want, not what you think you can or should have. Don't compromise. Don't be discouraged if you set a date to achieve a goal and it doesn't happen. It means that you have not mentally accepted it yet, or that the time is not right.

Listen while you sleep

Audio cassette programs can be used as an aid to clear away mental block and re-create new thought patterns.

Worrying about the the past keeps it alive, so watch your thoughts and use them constructively. There are many tapes of affirmations available, or you could make your own. Listening while driving your car is a good time, as we often slip into an Alpha state, so the message has a far greater impact.

When Lisa was young I constantly listened to tapes when driving, often when Lisa was asleep. She has certainly adopted many of the messages that she heard as part of her belief system. You do not need to consciously listen, you can talk, think, or do other things, and your mind will still absorb the message. You can even go to sleep—but not when driving—most cassettes will switch off automatically.

Most cassette programs are safe to listen to while driving, but there are some such as relaxation or meditation tapes, or anything relating to clearing mental blocks, that are best listened to in a safe relaxed setting.

Subliminal tapes—the easy way

Subliminal cassettes re-program the subconscious without any conscious effort on your part. Subliminal tapes cannot be heard. Usually the message is covered over by music or sound-waves, but the subconscious mind, which is constantly alert, still absorbs it.

In the United States subliminal tapes were used to reduce shoplifting. When the message 'don't steal' was used, the incidence of shoplifting increased, because this acted as a reminder for some people to steal. When this message was changed to 'pay at the counter', the level of shoplifting was dramatically reduced. Flashing signs used for advertising have the same effect. Sometimes the message flicks on and off so quickly that we cannot read it, but the subconscious mind absorbs it anyway.

Subliminal tapes cannot be reproduced without special equipment and are not harmful. The message on the tape is usually printed on the cassette cover so that you know what is being said. The advantage of using this method is that you by-pass the conscious mind which often analyses and rejects a new message. The subconscious does not judge, therefore it will more readily accept a new message.

Don't worry if things go wrong

If you listen to a weight loss tape and you start eating more, or a quit smoking tape and you smoke more, this is merely resistance coming to the surface. I have often recommended Louise Hay's Self Healing tape for people wishing to clear mental block, and there have been some unusual reactions. When I first listened to it I felt depressed for two weeks, but perservered and eventually felt wonderful. One girl couldn't sleep, another developed numerous ailments, while one ran into the back of a car. Be prepared if you want to change a deep-seated pattern. It may not be easy initially, but the end result is worth the effort. If the experience is too uncomfortable, take a break and try again a few weeks later.

We create mental images of what we want whilst in a relaxed Alpha state. Forcing or struggling will only bring you back to a conscious level. Try breaking the goal into small pieces which your mind can readily accept.

Meditation

To establish any new habit, you need to make a commitment and set aside a time of day when you will not be interrupted. At work, if I am feeling drained or looking for a particular solution, I tell the receptionist to hold calls and not interrupt me for ten minutes. If your work does not permit this, you may be able to pull over to the side of the road for ten minutes on your way home from work. Meditation classes can help, as can yoga or tai chi, as they all strengthen concentration skills.

It doesn't really matter if you use a method of relaxation, such as consciously being aware of your body allowing every muscle to relax, or you meditate by fixing your gaze on a candle. Whatever works for you is best. What you are aiming for is to slow the brainwaves, but there are other benefits as well.

During meditation the level of oxygen required by the body decreases. Metabolism slows down and the body's energy resources are used less. Blood lactate levels fall and this reduces anxiety. Meditation is rejuvenating, so if you feel tired and washed out, try it. If you want peace of mind learn to meditate. Encourage your whole family to join you, including children. No words can describe how wonderful meditation feels.

Ideally you need a quiet environment, but once you are proficient at this art, you may be able to shut out noise. To begin with, have as few distractions as possible. Get comfortable, it doesn't matter what position you take as long as you're not going to be distracted by tight shoes or uncomfortable clothing. Take off shoes, glasses and belts, if possible. I usually sit in a place where I carry out no other activity, so that I'm less likely to be distracted. I prefer to have no parts of the body crossed to allow energy to flow freely through me.

The method I prefer is as follows:

Sit quietly.
Close your eyes.
Breathe deeply. Focus you attention on one thing, which could be your breathing or a word of your choice.
Allow any thoughts that enter your mind to slide away on a limp piece of silk. Keep bringing your focus back to your breathing.
Breathe out tension—Breathe in peace and harmony.
Come back to consciousness slowly, counting from number ten backwards.

Continue with this method for a few days before doing any visualisation. If you try to do too much at once you'll only get tense and defeat your purpose.

If you have never meditated before or have been unsuccessful, listen to a guided relaxation or meditation tape. All you do is sit back and follow instructions. Like acquiring any new skill, it takes practice, so don't give up because you feel uncomfortable at first.

Once you feel comfortable meditating start creating visual images. You can visualise a screen with your life being played out on it like a movie, or, you could create a safe place—a room or a place in the countryside. Start by seeing yourself the way you want to be, smiling, happy, enjoying life and looking good. See yourself doing the things you want to do, with the people you want to be near. Feel the love and approval of these people.

Commit yourself to meditating once a day to begin with. Commence with five or ten minutes and gradually increase to half an hour a day. Meditation is addictive in the best possible way. At first the mind chatters and emotions rise; some people get irritated, some fall asleep, others are aware of what is going on around them. Those who persevere find that they soon slip into a wonderful warm safe space, where a feeling of peace, bliss even, envelopes you.

CHAPTER 8

Keys to success

Want money? Then give some away

Life is like a boomerang, what you give out you get back, so ensure that your actions match your desires. The best way to eradicate lack in any form—money, love, ideas, employment—is to give. Giving opens the doors to receiving.

Look again at your life. Are you the person you want to be and do you give what you want to receive? There is nothing wrong with giving in the expectation of receiving what you want.

Every one of us has something of value to give. If you want to receive money back, then give money. If you cannot give money, there are other ways to give:

* if seeking promotion, give more than you are paid for
* if self employed, give your clients real service
* if unemployed, work voluntarily
* listen when someone needs to talk
* give the Taxation Department the correct amount of taxes
* clean out your cupboards and give unused clothing and items away.
* recycle glass and paper products

My secretary, Valerie, and I have been friends for many years. She arrived at work one day feeling upset over something that had happened overnight and said, 'I need to type the book today, to lift me up'. The section she was typing was on giving. I mentioned that my daughter Lisa was feeling down in the doldrums and Valerie suggested that we do something to lift her spirits, asking, 'What can we give her?'

Without giving it much thought I said 'What she'd really like is a trip to Italy to meet up with her girlfriend, but she hasn't got the money'. Valerie said 'That's it, we'll go halves in a plane ticket to Italy for her'. I was stunned, as I wasn't thinking of anything of such magnitude, nor did I expect such generosity. But I believe in practising what I preach, so we decided to go ahead and Valerie said, 'Just think what will come back to us'.

We rang Lisa at work and she was flabbergasted, excited and confused all at once. She kept saying 'Are you sure?'. The rest of the day was spent making travel bookings and ringing Lisa to confirm things. What a difference! What started out being a depressing day, suddenly turned into a day full of excitement. Valerie and I remember well the days when we were both living on the pension. Now we both do the things that we enjoy.

You don't need money to have the things you want. Giving works. If you don't like something that has been given to you, accept it graciously, then pass it on. Keep the flow going. When I was on the pension, three-quarters of the amount I received went on rent, which left us with very little over, but I decided to give monthly to the Bangladesh appeal that was on at that time. It wasn't long before our circumstances improved.

Among my clients I have noticed that the ones who give freely are always provided for. I do stress 'give freely' as I have seen women manipulated out of money by family members. Then, it is not true giving, but playing the victim.

Some people will give freely to all types of people, but when it comes to paying taxes they go to incredible lengths to avoid paying. People hide large amounts of cash in their homes, or in safety deposit boxes, afraid to use the money for fear of being discovered. This type of action only encourages the belief that there is 'not enough'.

Giving is a way of demonstrating your trust that there will always be enough for you, the Tax Department and everyone else. If you believe you deserve abundance, then you cannot act out of fear, otherwise your words and actions are out of sync. Trust is putting your beliefs into action. Giving for its own sake makes you feel good.

Expect to receive, it is everyone's right, but you cannot stipulate the source. When giving, give freely with no strings attached. Most of us think we give unconditionally, but how would you react to the following situation? Imagine you came into $50 000 unexpectedly and decided to give the entire amount to a friend in financial difficulty. Your friend is delighted and immediately sets a match to the $50,000 and says 'I always wanted to have money to burn'. How would you react? The reality is that most gifts have expectations attached to them.

Make way for the new by letting go of the old ideas, clean out your cupboards in expectation of replacing items with what you want. When you cling to the old, you hinder your own progress. Nature abhors a vacuum.

Is ten a magic number?

The ancient laws considered ten a magic number of increase. Today much is still written about giving 10 per cent of all you receive. Supposedly it will come back to you tenfold. This practice is commonly known as tithing. Prosperous nationalities in early times, such as the Babylonians, Persians, Greeks, Romans, all practised tithing.

Some churches encourage their congregations to tithe a tenth of their income to the church. To the contemporary woman this may seem preposterous, particularly if you don't agree with the teachings of churches, but does it work?

Some say yes, others no. My own experience has neither proved nor disproved it. I believe that in some cases unconscious beliefs hinder some people from receiving.

Tithing simply means sharing what you have with others and sharing means we could totally eliminate poverty as it exists today. If there was less need, money spent on welfare, pensions and subsidies would be unnecessary, taxes could be cut and everyone would benefit. Don't wait until you are prosperous to start tithing. Everyone can give something.

Expect to receive

Financial freedom can be obstructed by people who don't know when or how to receive. The ideal is to maintain a balance between giving and receiving. If someone offers to do something for you, or gives you money, accept graciously.

Refusing to receive simply deprives another person of an opportunity to give. It is saying that the gift has no value to you.

On one occasion I was preparing a financial plan for a client who was quite well off and wanted to help her niece to buy a home of her own. She decided to allocate a certain amount for her niece to use for this purpose, and whether the money was repaid or not was of no consequence to her.

The niece, quite unaware of her aunt's intentions, also sought financial advice from me. Her goal was to buy her own home, but she did not have quite enough for a deposit. Coincidentally the exact amount needed was the same as her aunt had set aside for her. Her aunt's plan was obviously something that was meant to be, but I was not at liberty to mention anything at this stage.

Soon after, the aunt offered the money, with no strings attached. The niece refused. She believed that she could not afford to repay the money and refused to accept it as a gift. Her pride benefited no-one, because since then real estate prices have doubled and she could have bought and sold and repaid her aunt a handsome profit and still been ahead.

If there is no-one in your life to give to you, then give to yourself. Take time out for a day all to yourself, or a beauty treatment. As you continue in this pattern, other people will enter your life who want to give to you.

Some of the most giving people in our society simply cannot allow others to do something for them, and this is particularly the case for people who work in caring professions such as social workers, doctors and counsellors. This can result in burnout and they become of little value to themselves and others. When you lead a balanced life you will never suffer burnout no matter how hard you work.

When I first began having regular massages I really didn't have the money to spare. The business that has been generated in referrals from this source has been sufficient to pay for massages for the next five years. Giving and receiving are inseparable twins.

If you follow the principle of forgetting the 'how' and concentrating on 'what' you want, then you cannot refuse an opportunity when it arrives. The only exception to this is when someone is trying to manipulate you, or to make you feel indebted to them, in which case say a definite 'no'.

Persistence pays off

'Often failure is success trying to be born in a bigger way', says Catherine Ponder in her book, *The Dynamic Laws of Prosperity*[10]. When failure is imminent, many people give up, instead of holding on a little longer, or looking for alternatives. This is the critical eleventh hour, when old thought patterns rise to the surface. Don't give in. There is so much more to be gained by eradicating them.

On the other hand, when success is imminent, a subtle kind of fear may occur. Questions, such as how your life will change, or whether you will still be the same person, enter your mind. Many women become pregnant at this point in their career, as a way of opting out without admitting failure.

It is relatively easy to aim for a goal that is a long way off. Only when that dream looks like becoming a reality does fear enter. This is where you can sabotage yourself if you are not aware of what is happening.

I've often heard people say 'What have I done?' when their life is about to change dramatically. This is a perfectly normal reaction and will pass in time, if the feeling is not given too much attention.

Everything can also go wrong simply because people expect it to. Have you ever said 'I knew it was too good to be true, something had to go wrong'? This is simply an old belief that needs to be replaced.

If efforts are half-hearted or spasmodic, the results will reflect this. Are you committed to achieving your goal? If not, replace it with one that really excites you. In one of my workshops, participants were completing the checklist at the back of this chapter. When it came to the question 'are you prepared to put in the effort to achieve this goal?', one woman who wanted a red BMW Sports said 'Of course not'. Obviously that goal had insufficient pulling power for her, and that is perfectly O.K.

The idea is to aim for what you really want. If you go the second mile, there can come a time when you feel exhausted and worn out, but if you really want something and push yourself that little bit further, you will get your second wind. Keep your focus on the main objective and give yourself little rewards along the way. Disappointments only dissipate your energy, so feel the emotion, then let it go.

Enthusiasm often motivates people to jump into get-rich-quick schemes and they become so fired up with making money that they want it NOW. One man brought along a savings plan that had been recommended to him. The salesman had quoted returns that had been earned prior to the stock-market crash, and told him he would make a huge amount of money very quickly. He must have had some doubts, or he would not have asked me for a second opinion. I explained that the charges on this plan were very high, amounting to the first two years' savings, and that the real return averaged over a few years was not what the salesman quoted. As this client had only been self-employed for six months, I suggested that he hold off any such action to ensure his income was established first. I also put forward some alternative plans he could take once he knew what his regular base income would be.

He decided that he had to do something now, and that the get-rich-quick scheme was preferable. I imagine that by the time two years are up, he will get tired of seeing no money in his account and will stop saving into this plan—thereby literally throwing away that money. I have seen countless people take this course of action, and all they've achieved is to remain in the same situation.

Plodders, the ones who refuse to give up, often make the most money in the end. That doesn't mean that money or investments have to be boring. It does mean that those who are prepared to persevere and save, or follow a plan of action through to completion, are the ones who will prosper. When it seems the least likely, the floodgates of abundance will open for you. Be ready to accept it.

Staying focused

Successful people all have one thing in common. They are able to focus all of their energies on a specific goal.

Energy when focused is very powerful. Misdirected energy takes you nowhere.

We have all seen sports people achieve great heights through focusing their energies on winning a single event. On an everyday level most people just aren't that committed. Fortunately you don't have to be, but you do need to keep your mind on what you wish to achieve. You need to develop tunnel vision until such time as this desire becomes firmly entrenched in your mind, and the time this takes will differ for each individual.

Valerie is not at all ambitious or career-minded. She has very few goals, just wanting an easy life with little responsibility. Her one great love is travel. She likes to go overseas twice a year, and does, although she works part-time and does not have a lot of money. Valerie's greatest asset is that she can totally focus on what she wants. She refuses to worry. Because she is so cheerful people like to go away with her and usually pay her way as well.

She constantly calls in at travel agents, and always has her next trip or two planned. This year she had three trips in four months, two overseas and one interstate. One trip she paid for herself, another was paid for by a friend and the third, she won, and she always travels in comfort. As well as remaining focused, Valerie is very generous, often giving to others and she has no trouble accepting free holidays.

Lisa is also very focused, and living with a person who has this characteristic has its drawbacks. Lisa too has a love of travelling and is constantly talking about her trips, sometimes nearly driving me crazy, but how can I complain? She is either saving, spending, buying or looking at the next trip, and it works. At age twenty, she is about to take her fourth overseas trip, and will have visited sixteen countries.

When you scatter your energies, results will be scattered. In business, attempts at marketing or organisation are often sporadic. Some firms say 'let's try that' and if no results are obtained in a short time, they change direction, only to repeat the pattern. No wonder they don't succeed. If your personal affairs are a mess, with unpaid bills all over the house and ten different bank accounts, you will only get back confusion.

We scatter our energies when we talk to too many people about our plans. Talkers often dissipate their energy this way and don't even get to the starting point. We scatter our energies when we take on too many projects at once; hold onto resentment; dither; get caught up in everyday problems; have self-doubts or worry.

One of the major causes of scattered energies is constantly looking for solutions. Problems are a part of life, there is no denying that, but to constantly talk about them, or waste energy running around searching for an answer only compounds the difficulties. Get into the habit of not talking about problems unless it becomes essential, such as when you have a problem with another which needs to be communicated, or if you require professional advice. If you need the release of talking, do it, then let it go. You can stay focused by setting a daily routine, maintaining order in your affairs, being open to receive from unexpected channels and replacing fear-filled thoughts with positive affirmations.

Letting go

The things in life that aren't so important are mostly the ones that come the easiest. Have you ever applied for a job and not really cared if you got it or not? That's usually the one you'll get. But the job you really want will often elude you.

When we want something badly we cling to it, often becoming fearful that we won't get it. The vibrations that we send off are full of fear. Without realising it, other people pick up our vibrations and react accordingly, often bringing about the very thing we fear.

Most people would have had the experience of trying to coerce someone to do something only to have them resist, and do just the opposite. Children are particularly adept at this reaction. Then, just when you decide it's not worth the effort to persuade them, they do what you wanted them to do all along.

One of my clients is going through a difficult divorce. She is entitled to a large divorce settlement but is afraid that she will not get it. At least once a day she rings me, as well as her solicitor, accountant, and numerous friends. She keeps going over the same things time and again, and it is costing her a fortune in professional fees.

I have suggested many times that she has done all she can, now she has to let go of the result, but she cannot. As a consequence, a large proportion of the divorce settlement will go on unnecessary fees, and she may not be any better off. She has also caused herself a lot of unnecessary anxiety.

It's easy to say let go but not always so easy to do in reality, yet there will be no long-lasting peace or happiness until you learn this most important step. The inability to let go is only fear reflected from subconscious beliefs, in which case you will have to do some more work on changing those beliefs. Are your actions based on fear or faith?

Once your subconscious has been impressed with a certain image you can easily let it go, you don't even have to visualise or affirm anymore, it is already yours. However, you may get something different to what you asked for.

A woman wanted to buy a certain house but everything went wrong. The buyers for her house withdrew, she could not afford bridging finance, there were problems with a shared driveway. Still, she wanted this particular house desperately and in her mind she could see herself living there. The sale fell through. Not long after, another property came along that was far more suitable and had no problems. Everything ran smoothly this time and she was so grateful that she did not get her first choice.

Letting go of the past

The past is gone, and clinging to events, people or expectations only hinders your success today. James and Betty struggled all their lives raising a large family on a fixed income. The one good point was that they lived in a beautiful old mansion that had been inherited, except that it was a tremendous drain on their finances.

Once the children left home James and Betty sold their house for an enormous sum and moved to a smaller one. There was plenty of money for anything that they wanted, yet James could not quite believe it. He still acted poor, leaving bills unpaid and watching every penny. Instead of enjoying financial freedom today, he held on to the past.

Letting go of a person can be particularly painful but when a relationship is finished there is no other choice. The same applies when someone dies. By all means grieve, talk if it helps, but after a reasonable period pick up the pieces and move on.

Letting go of control

There are many people who only feel secure when they are in control. Although they may have the best intentions, and the best interest of others at heart, this often turns into manipulation. For instance, I have had mothers say to me' how can I make my son or daughter do your course?' You can't. You can encourage, but cannot force your will upon another, even your children. Nor can you mentally manipulate someone to change by using mind powers. By all means visualise people happy and contented, but let go of how they become that way.

When visualising or affirming for yourself, see the end

result, not how you are going to get it. Ask for what you want, but be prepared for not always getting it, as there may be something better for you. This happened to me when I wanted a particular job.

At the interview I was told that I had the job, but they had made prior arrangements to see one more person. A few days later I received a phone call to say they had accepted the other person. I was annoyed and disappointed, believing that I was perfect for the job. I had a lot of trouble mentally letting go of that job and kept expecting them to ring and say the other person hadn't worked out and it was mine.

Twelve months later the same man rang and offered me another position which led to my current one. Once I knew more about the firm I realised that the original job would not have suited me at all and there would have been a personality clash. That would have eliminated my opportunity to do the work I really love.

When something is meant for you things fall into place of their own accord. If everything goes wrong then it may be your unconscious beliefs coming to the surface, or, it may be your intuition pointing you in another direction. The best guidance you can get comes from your own inner voice. If you allow it to guide you, you will always be in the right place at the right time.

I don't always find it easy to let go, so I sometimes use a technique that was recommended to me. In a state of meditation, visualise your goal, then imagine placing this goal and all the people concerned with it into a pink bubble and let it go. See the bubble float off to the clouds like a balloon. Keep doing this until you feel that you mean it. You can then cease visualising and affirming, knowing that what is rightfully yours, either the image you've created, or something better, will come to you.

Sometimes we insist on having our dreams fulfilled right now, and sometimes the time is not right. I had just moved into a larger office, paid out for the telephone system to be installed and for extra furniture and signed a new lease. Within weeks I was told that the building had been sold and was given two months' notice. Although I had signed the lease, the owners said that they had not signed their copy. I was fuming.

At first I thought of taking legal action but decided that there was little point and I must be meant to go elsewhere. I searched for weeks but found nothing to my liking, so reluctantly I took up an offer from the owners to relocate to an office on the other side of the harbour. My main concern was that I would lose business once I was away from the central business district.

I couldn't have been more mistaken. Rather than lose business, it increased. Parking was easier for clients and I got the office that I had always visualised, with harbour views. It was on a different side of the harbour, but the view was spectacular.

Within a short period I moved house to the other side of the harbour as well. Instead of taking an hour to reach the office it now takes twenty minutes, which has proved to be a Godsend, especially since having my baby, Laura. Now I would never move my office back to the city. As a bonus the new owners offered me half rent for six months and because Telecom made a number of errors when installing the new phones, I wasn't charged for that as well. I made a profit.

If your dream involves another person and many do, even in a non-personal way, then the other person involved may have to do something first. If you have ever searched for your dream home to no avail, maybe you have to wait until the current owners sell. Once you feel confident in your own mind that you have done all you can, and you can feel that it is already yours, forget it.

Daily routine

We learn by repetition, and acquire new habits by being consistent in our efforts. To be financially free, establish a routine that becomes a part of your daily life.

A daily routine could consist of a reading or study time. A period of meditation can become a permanent part of your life, a chance to relax, as well as giving you the opportunity to create mental images of your life the way you want it to be. This gives you time for reading or researching, and a time to dream and create. This routine could take ten minutes or half an hour, or even longer. Half an hour a day is not much. Most of us waste at least that each day, but over a year it adds up to 182 hours. That is 182 hours of focused energy on what you want. Who said they had no time?

Make a time clock and write in the times of day that you will devote to achieving your goal. Put it in a prominent place, so that others in the family will know that this is your time.

Be prepared to act

Use your time constructively and make a commitment to yourself. I cannot stress this enough. There are people who go from course to course, looking for someone else to solve their problems. Once they finish, they do nothing and they wonder why their life has not changed. All they have done is gained little more than entertainment, and a big dent in their savings.

There are no easy answers. Affirmations work, visualisation works, but you have to be prepared. I could not visualise this book in print if I was not prepared to put in the time writing it. The powers of your mind are not magic, they can only work WITH you. Corporations spend thousands on staff training to motivate and train staff, but it counts for nothing if the individual does not act when opportunity comes.

Taking action at the appropriate time is the difference between success and failure.

Complete the checklist at the end of this chapter. Do the exercises that you feel are appropriate for you and set a daily routine that will take you towards your goal.

Checklist

Do you want the goal that you have set enough to put in the effort to achieve it?

_____

What obstacles stand in your way?

_____

_____

_____

Have you gained anything by being in your present situation?

_____

_____

_____

If so, are you prepared to either give this gain up, or find a more positive way of achieving the same benefit?

_____

_____

_____

Are your words and actions in alignment with your dreams?

_____

_____

_____

Are you focusing on what you want, rather than the problems surrounding it, or how to get it?

_____

_____

_____

Are you blocking yourself from receiving?

_____

_____

_____

Have you set a daily routine?

_____

_____

_____

Summary

Knowledge is power. Discovering and acknowledging your own power is the beginning of financial freedom. To create the life you want simply:

* Program your subconscious so that it will support (not sabotage) your dreams.

* Focus on what you want, not how to get it.
* Be open to receive from all sources.

Having done this you need to put your affairs in order, and take the next step by learning some basic skills about money management. You may find you already have all you need, and it's a simple matter of using it more efficiently. Or, you may wish to acquire wealth, in which case you need to be prepared. You cannot plan for wealth without knowing what to do with it when it comes.

PART TWO

Changing your habits

CHAPTER 9

Order in your affairs

Recently I attended a gardening course. My only prior knowledge of gardening was what I had picked up from my parents and from trial and error with indoor plants. The first week I felt totally overwhelmed, particularly when the teacher said that she would use the correct botanical terms throughout the course. It occurred to me that this must be how many of my clients feel when they first seek advice about investments. After a number of weeks I understood what the teacher was saying, and felt good about myself and the new knowledge that I'd gained. Acquiring new investment skills is a similar process to learning about gardening.

Like my gardening teacher, I intend using the correct terminology throughout this section, as you will need to understand it when you seek advice. I'll explain the meaning of these terms as I go, but there is also an appendix that includes information on various financial terms.

Everyone who has a savings account is an investor, so don't be turned off by thinking you have to have a large amount of money. Some organisations differentiate between savers and investors, but it's just semantics, and for our purposes, everyone is an investor. Whether you have a lot of money or a little, you need to establish order in your affairs.

The mere mention of anything relating to money management turns many people off. They have preconceived ideas that they are hopeless at maths—poor money managers—too stupid to understand—frightened by the word investments. Many people regard books on practical financial matters to be dull and boring, and they can be. This is not another one of those books. Money can be fun, seeing your own money grow is even more fun. But you do need some basic knowledge on money management and investments. My challenge is to make this subject interesting for you too.

Valerie, my secretary, commented on how her daughter is doing poorly at maths and said 'I was hopeless at maths too. I don't understand anything when it comes to figures'. When I asked if she understood the financial plans she types for me, she said 'Oh yes, but that's different, you make it so easy'. The only difference involved is that because she is relaxed and there is no pressure on her to perform, she doesn't automatically put up her mental barrier.

So, let's explode myth number one by stressing that you don't have to be good with figures to make money. Myth number two is that you should already know all about money management. I don't know it all. I have learnt though, that to be good at my job, I need to know where to access information, rather than try to carry it all around in my head. Men are the worst offenders. So many feel that they should know about insurance, superannuation, taxation, investments and so on. Very few people do. They are specialist fields. I do know basic taxation laws, but when it comes to something out of the ordinary, I refer to a specialist.

Because of this reluctance to admit to their lack of knowledge, people, particularly men, either don't ask questions, or resist taking advice. They are more likely to be sold products that benefit the salesperson rather than the buyer. Knowing what questions to ask can be a stumbling block, but this can be overcome by gaining a little knowledge.

People with little money often have no idea where their money goes. As a general rule these clients cannot give me loan details, or monthly repayments. At times they do not know their gross incomes. They suffer from the ostrich syndrome. It's easier to bury their heads in the sand than face reality. Usually they are looking for someone to take over their problems.

There is no order in their affairs.

On the other hand, some people, usually those with substantial sums, can go to the other extreme. They know where every cent goes. Their records are in perfect order, but they watch their money too closely. They constantly check, and re-check, never sure that they have made the right decision, afraid to spend, in case there isn't enough. They are like a child who plants a seed in the garden, then digs it up to see if it is growing.

Order in affairs is vital, and so too is balance.

Where to start

Everyone needs to know the following:
(a) Gross and net income
(b) Marginal tax rate
(c) Cost of living, e.g. rent, phone, electricity, food, car expenses
(c) Loan details, particularly the interest rate being paid
(d) Number of bank accounts
(e) Insurance details
(f) Superannuation details
(g) Investment details

It may just seem to be common sense, but there are many people who do not know how much they earn, or what it costs them to live. You need to know your marginal tax rate, so that you are aware of what tax you will incur on any savings or investments. This may be a deciding factor for choosing investments.

Loan details are important, as interest rates vary with differing types of loans. If you are paying off numerous credit cards, it may be to your advantage to consolidate by obtaining a personal loan, so that you have only one monthly repayment.

Too many bank accounts can cost you money, and you scatter energy keeping track of them.

Superannuation funds have many variables that will affect the amount you receive. So it is in your best interest to know these details rather than find out on retirement that you could have received much more.

Many investors do not understand their investments. This is a grave mistake. Although you may not be an expert you need to know if your investment will fluctuate in value, how risky it is, and whether you pay tax on it. Never be shy about asking these questions, even if you have held the investment for some time.

Maintaining records

It is not necessary to set up a filing cabinet, write up ledgers, or install a home computer. Any easy-to-manage system will do. I usually recommend that clients buy a concertina folder and label the sections according to records kept. I have mine labelled: legal papers, investments, insurance, warranties, tax returns, certificate (birth etc.) and miscellaneous. Once set up, this system is the easiest in the world to manage. I just drop everything behind the appropriate slot, and I know where to go if I need something.

As accounts come in, either pay them straight away, or place into an 'accounts to be paid' folder. Once a month, or each pay day, pay the accounts, then file them in an envelope, or folder, entitled 'accounts paid'. I keep separate 'accounts paid' files for each financial year, and when it comes to tax time I just go through this folder. It is only basic commonsense, but only a minority of people use any sort of system at all.

In my first business venture I was employed by a woman to spend a day in her home, setting up a filing system. This was not for business purposes, just normal household records. After a whole day I had barely made a dent in the mountain of papers that she had. Receipts dated back twenty years. Bills were all over the place. Cheques, still in envelopes, had been shoved in files, there were hundreds of dollars that had never been banked. Money thrown away because of lack of organisation.

If you are really orderly you could make up a list showing details of where your Will is kept, and who your executor is. Other details could include: bank accounts; investment certificates; life insurance; superannuation; name and addresses of financial advisers; accountant; solicitor; where title deeds are kept; and who holds the mortgages. A copy of this list can be given to another family member, or alternatively you can tell someone close to you where it is kept.

The buck stops with you

As much as you may like to, you cannot pass responsibility for your financial affairs completely over to another person. Ultimately you are the person that is responsible to the Tax Department or any other legal body, as one man found out the hard way.

Richard Bach's books have delighted thousands of people like me. He was just an ordinary man who wanted to fly planes, write books, and find his soulmate. While he was travelling around America in search of his soulmate, he ran out of money. When he rang his publisher to see if there was money available from his book sales, he discovered that he had become instantly rich. Millions of dollars rich. He didn't know how to be a rich person. He thought he might read a book on the subject, so tried the local library. He found books on how to make money, but not how to cope with sudden wealth. He said:

'I was drowning in money. People around the world were reading the book, buying copies of other books I'd written. Money from every book sale came from the publisher back to me.'[11]

He didn't want to be bothered with money, so he handed control over to a financial manager and said 'It's your business, full-time and I'm out of it!' He lost money, but continued to ignore all the warning signs, he didn't want the responsibility.

The next thing he heard, the Internal Revenue Service wanted a million dollars in back taxes. He thought it was a mistake, a simple matter not to be taken too seriously. When he was asked what his annual income was he hadn't a clue. It could have been $50 000, or $2 000 000. His financial manager told him that he had lost all his money, and was sorry. His lawyer said that he shouldn't owe a cent, but because they missed the Internal Revenue Services' deadline, it was now too late to appeal.

Meanwhile the Internal Revenue Service had won a judgement by default and demanded payment of $1 000 000 in back taxes. Richard offered cash down and the balance to be paid over five years, from projected earnings on future book sales. They refused, wanting only payment in full. They continued to refuse all offers. After four years of fighting, Richard Bach filed for bankruptcy. Four years wasted, no books written, and a million dollars lost. An expensive way to learn a lesson.

In the end each one of us is responsible for our own affairs. You can allow family and friends to help you, you can pay for financial advice, but ultimately the consequences of all decisions come back to you.

Once you've established some order, you need to know where your money goes. This applies to everyone. Knowing where your money goes allows you to make choices. Do you really want to spend every cent you earn, or would you prefer to put some of it towards a larger goal? Do you want the icecream today, or the bicycle tomorrow?

The easiest way to find out where your money goes is to carry a notebook with you for a month and write down everything that you spend. You may be surprised at where your money really goes. Even if you find this exercise depressing, it is something you need to know. Knowledge allows you to make choices. Staying in the dark takes you nowhere.

Begin with a budget

If you live beyond your means, you can take practical steps to control your spending by making a budget. I personally don't like budgets that are too rigid. A budget should be as individual as you are.

Budgets, like diets, need only be adopted for short periods. Once your affairs are in order you can adopt a more flexible approach. A budget can be broken up into various categories such as: household expenses, travel, personal expenditure and so on. Once you gather all your figures, you can then assess if there is balance between the categories. Is a large proportion of your income being spent to repay loans as a result of compulsive spending? Are you living within your means? Have you allowed money for your prosperity item and for fun? Have you put yourself first by allocating some savings?

I have observed that usually those with financial problems have a tendency to throw money away on trivial items like magazines, stationery, or gadgets, that are often not used. If you have to spend every cent you lay your hands on, it may be indicative of a deeper problem. Spending uncontrollably is not acting prosperously.

A good budget allows for the unexpected and it should always be flexible. Allowance should be made for some fun, otherwise you'll never stick to it.

Budgeting Tips

* Make a budget to suit your pay period. If paid monthly, then calculate all costs on a monthly basis. If paid weekly, estimate all expenses on a weekly basis. Don't just multiply weekly expenses by four, as some months have five weeks. Multiply by 52, then divide by 12, to bring it to a monthly figure.
* Revise your budget at least once a year.
* Make the first item on your budget your luxury money, for something that makes you feel prosperous. This money can be spent on yourself to cultivate a prosperity consciousness. Place regular savings towards your goals at the top of your list as well.
* The attached budget planner divides expenditure into various categories. Check that these categories are not out of balance. You may find that all of your income goes on your children and other people, and not enough on you. Look for patterns of spending. Are they the way you want them to be?
* Allow for incidentals, such as magazines, dry cleaning, subscriptions, sport, outings, presents, hairdresser. These are things we tend to forget.

Having made your budget, add up all expenses and subtract from your income. Do you have a positive or negative cash flow? If you have a positive cash flow then you may wish to allocate this money towards your goal. If your cash flow is negative and your expenses come to more than you earn, then you will have to reassess your spending habits, or find ways to increase your income.

There is nothing like writing a book to make you look at your own affairs. Having recently become very environmentally conscious, I've changed a lot of the products that I buy in the supermarket, and have resorted to some of the old fashioned cleaning methods. My supermarket bill has dropped by $50 a week.

A good idea is to calculate how much of your money

goes towards paying regular bills, and open a bill-paying account just for this purpose. If you save regularly into your bill-paying account you need never worry again when a bill comes in. This allows you to focus on what you want rather than on debts or bills.

For example, say your regular bills are:

Electricity	$150 a quarter	= $600pa
Telephone	$100 a quarter	= $400pa
Car Insurance		$500pa
Car Registration		$500pa
Car Maintenance		$500pa
Driver's Licence		$ 23pa
Rates (Council & Water)		$1200pa
Insurance (House & Contents)		$250pa
Insurance (Health)		$350pa
Subscriptions		$200pa
		$4523

Divide this figure by twelve, and you know that if you put $377 into a bill-paying account each month, you will always have enough to pay bills when they fall due. Instead of moaning about the bills that you have to pay, rejoice. Sound odd? Not really—if we didn't have the benefit of a home, or telephone, or car we wouldn't have these bills. How boring life would be.

Budget planner

PROSPERITY ITEM	ESTIMATED EXPENDITURE $
SAVINGS	
PERSONAL	
SUPERANNUATION	
OTHER	

HOUSEHOLD EXPENSES
RATES—WATER   _____
           COUNCIL   _____
RENT/MORTGAGE   _____
LEVY   _____
ELECTRICITY/GAS   _____
TELEPHONE   _____
INSURANCE—HOUSE   _____
           CONTENTS   _____
           OTHER   _____
MAINTENANCE   _____
LAWNS/GARDENS   _____
POOL   _____
FOOD (INCLUDE LUNCHES,
     MILK, BREAD, TAKE-
     AWAYS)   _____
ALCOHOL

TRANSPORT
CAR—PETROL   _____
     INSURANCE   _____
     REGISTRATION   _____
     REPAIRS/MAINTENANCE   _____
     NRMA   _____
     DRIVER'S LICENCE   _____
     FARES   _____
     TAXIS   _____

DEBTS
CREDIT CARDS   _____
CHARGE ACCOUNTS   _____
PERSONAL LOANS   _____
HIRE PURCHASE   _____
FAMILY/FRIENDS   _____
OTHER   _____

PERSONAL EXPENDITURE
DRY CLEANING   _____
CLOTHES   _____
HAIRDRESSER   _____
BEAUTY SALON/MAKE UP   _____

HEALTH FOODS/VITAMINS _____
CIGARETTES _____
MEDICAL INSURANCE _____
CHIROPRACTOR/
    NATUROPATH _____
LOTTERIES/GAMBLING _____
MASSAGE _____
LIFE INSURANCE _____
MAGAZINE/NEWSPAPERS _____
BOOKS/RECORDS _____
ENTERTAINMENT _____
HOLIDAYS _____
MEMBERSHIPS/
    SUBSCRIPTIONS _____
HOBBIES/COURSES _____
SPORT/GYM _____
OTHER _____

OTHER PEOPLE
CHILDREN'S LESSONS _____
CHILDREN'S POCKET
    MONEY _____
PRESENTS _____
CLOTHES _____
DONATIONS _____
CHILD MINDING _____
ACTIVITIES _____
SCHOOL FEES _____
OTHER _____

TOTAL

Do you know your net worth? You can find out by listing all your assets and liabilities.

LIABILITIES (What you owe)
List total amounts owing on:
    Mortgage   _____
    Car   _____
    Personal Loan   _____
    Credit Cards   _____
    Charge Cards   _____
    Other   _____

ASSETS (What you own)
Do not include personal items
such as jewellery, furniture.
    House   _____
    Car   _____
    Savings   _____
    Investments   _____
    Superannuation   _____
    Collectables (Artworks, etc.)   _____

Deduct your liabilities
from your assets   _____

Net Worth

If your liabilities come to more than you own, then you need to concentrate on clearing your debts, whilst at the same time saving small amounts. Or, see a financial counsellor.

Conversely, if you discover that you are worth more than you thought, it often gives you the motivation to build on this wealth.

CHAPTER 10

Build a strong foundation

Kristene was paying $4500 in interest each year on credit card debts and personal loans. Judy was losing $1000 a year in interest by having ten small bank accounts, rather than one larger one earning a higher interest rate. Sue and John were able to save $25 000 on their mortgage repayments, simply by increasing repayments by $3.69 each week.

In order to be financially free you need to build a strong foundation. You can start by reassessing bank accounts and understanding the credit system, insurance, investments and knowing the amount of tax you pay.

Choosing a bank account

Having too many accounts is a common practice. Accounts can cost money and often a higher interest can be earned by amalgamating these savings into one or two accounts. Have an everyday account, a special purpose account, and a bill-paying account. Unless your circumstances are unusual, you will rarely need more than three.

Meg attended a Financially Free course, and made an appointment for a private consultation afterwards. Before the date came around she cancelled. She said that when she was getting her papers ready to see me she discovered that she had umpteen small bank accounts, and said 'I then realised that every time I've ever made any extra money I quickly hid it away by opening another account. I'm going to reorganise myself and get comfortable with having, and spending money'.

There are no hard and fast rules for choosing the right bank, building society or credit union. The financial world is extremely competitive and products are constantly changing. Check that there are no hidden fees, and check interest rates periodically.

Check that the charges on your bank statement agree with what has been quoted. A common practice among some banks is to quote one rate, but when the loan application goes to the area branch for approval this rate can be increased. Your bank manager is discouraged from telling you of this.

I heard of another woman who wouldn't even consider changing banks because they always treated her so well, offering her coffee whenever she came into the branch. No wonder, she had in excess of a hundred thousand dollars sitting in a savings account earning only four per cent interest. The bank could afford it!

The following guidelines may assist you in choosing a bank and an account:

Make sure the bank manager knows you, as you may need his help one day. You can make an appointment to introduce yourself.

Check all charges, particularly cheque accounts. Some accounts make no charges if a minimum balance is held in the account, but you may make more money by investing elsewhere and paying the charges.

Check interest rates periodically, don't leave large amounts in low interest accounts.

Check interest rates on overdrafts or loans periodically as well.

Don't lock into fixed interest investments if you don't need the income. Investigate investments that offer capital growth.

Ensure that your bank is accessible. You may sabotage yourself by carrying money around because you cannot get to the bank.

The credit trap

A financial plan that was set up five or ten years ago may not be the best one for today. It is a good idea to review your financial affairs once a year. Make a list of all liabilities including the balances owing on credit cards, loans and mortgages, the interest rate and the monthly repayment amount. Calculate how much you are paying in interest each year.

A balance of $10 000 on credit cards can cost $2200 a year in interest charges. Add this amount to any personal loan debts and interest on mortgage, and it can add up to a sizeable sum.

It is the very ease of readily available credit that leads people into the trap of over-spending. Prosperous people live within their means now, while endeavouring to raise their standard of living. Living beyond your means in the expectation of money coming from some mythical source is a dangerous habit.

If you are heavily indebted to credit cards, you may be better off applying for a consolidation loan, which involves only one monthly repayment, often at a lower rate of interest. This frees you from focusing on debts and allows you to concentrate on your goal. Cut up your credit cards, or put them away, otherwise you will only make things worse.

Credit can be a great asset as long as it is used wisely. Some types, if used carefully, attract no interest. Department stores often give up to ninety days free credit for larger items. Instead of using your credit card to purchase items such as video recorders, microwaves and so on, check with the credit department of the store to find out if you can open a ninety day account. Or, by taking note of the closing date when using your store charge card, you can have up to sixty days free credit.

How much is it costing you?

Finance companies make money out of people's ignorance. When I was looking for a car, the salesman wanted me to make a decision on the spot, and tried to persuade me to take out a loan with their finance company. When I asked about the interest rate, I was quoted 12 per cent. Sounds good on the surface, but I happened to know that this was not the current rate. What he quoted was 12 per cent flat, which equates to an interest rate of 23 per cent reducible, not nearly so attractive.

Flat interest is calculated on the full amount of the loan and the interest does not reduce as you make loan repayments. If you repaid the loan early you would still have to pay the full amount. Reducible interest means that as the balance owing decreases, so does the amount of interest you pay. Lenders are supposed to quote reducible interest rates, but as with our car salesman, I know this does not always happen.

It is essential to know the real cost of credit. Most people focus on the monthly repayments and don't consider the overall cost. If you are borrowing $10 000 and the monthly repayments are $243 a month over five years, the total cost to you is $14 600. Are you prepared to pay this? Multiply the term of the loan by the monthly repayment to ascertain the real cost.

Credit rating

Each time you apply for a loan, whether it is taken up or not, this information is recorded on your file with a credit bureau. Whenever you apply to rent through an estate agent or apply for a telephone, credit checks are generally carried out. That is how creditors know if you have a bad repayment history, or have not declared all debts on your application.

If you have been refused credit, or just want a copy of what is on your file you can apply to the bureau for one. Usually they require such information as full name and address for last five years, current driver's licence number, date of birth, and occupation. At time of writing this service costs $5. Information is kept on your file for five years, after which time it is deleted, so if you have made mistakes in the past, you are not stuck with them forever. If you find that the information on you is incorrect, then you can ask for your file to be amended.

Sources of credit

There are many sources of credit available, and probably more will become available as lenders compete for your business. Unlike years gone by, where you only applied to your bank for a loan, it is now wise to shop around, and don't be put off by one refusal. Some sources of credit available today are:

CREDIT CARDS/ STORE CHARGE CARDS	Interest rates are high. Pay out as quickly as possible.
PERSONAL LOANS	Interest rates vary with lenders and market conditions. Banks offer good customers a preferred rate but rarely advertise this. Finance companies usually charge the highest rates.

OVERDRAFTS	An ideal form of credit. Interest is only payable on the amount overdrawn. Not always easy to obtain, as banks try to direct you towards a personal loan which charges a higher interest rate.
INTEREST ONLY LOANS (BRIDGING FINANCE)	Often used to finance property purchases, or to settle new home purchase while waiting for existing property to be sold. Can be used for investment purposes. A fixed term is set after which time principal must be repaid or renegotiated.
FIRST MORTGAGE	Using property as security for loan. Often one of the cheapest forms of credit.
MORTGAGE LINE OF CREDIT	Allows you to draw up to a pre-determined amount for any purpose. A first mortgage is held by lender as security. Interest is only charged on outstanding balance.
CREDIT SALES	Replaced hire purchase. You are the owner of the goods which cannot be repossessed without a court order. Interest is usually high.
EXTENDED RETAIL CREDIT	Usually interest-free. A quarter of the purchase price is paid at time of purchase; the balance is payable over three monthly instalments. Varies from store to store.

The real cost of a mortgage

A home mortgage of $70 000, repayable over twenty-five years at an interest rate of 14 per cent costs $252 840. The monthly repayments are $842.80. Increase these repayments by $20.67 a week and the total repayments drop to $167 832. A saving of $85 008 and the repayment period is reduced by ten years.

Initially it's a good idea to take out a mortgage over a long period. This enables you to buy a home in a higher price bracket.

The first few years are often spent decorating or renovating and there are lots of unknown costs. However, after this time, or whenever you know your financial position more clearly, you can increase these repayments. A gradual increase of $5 a week each year, can save tens of thousands of dollars.

There are savings plans aimed at paying out the mortgage with a lump sum, but it is better to pay any additional savings directly off the mortgage. The disadvantage is that once this extra payment is made you cannot change your mind and call on the extra money.

One way around this is to have a mortgage line of credit. Using this type of loan you can have available to you up to 80 per cent of your property's value, depending upon your salary, and other commitments. The interest rate on this form of mortgage is usually higher than traditional mortgages.

Jim and Helen were both high income earners, with joint salaries in excess of $100 000 a year. They had a mortgage of $40 000 and savings of $30 000. I suggested that they change to a mortgage line of credit. Into this account they could place their $30 000 savings. This immediately reduced their mortgage interest, as they would only be paying interest on $10 000 instead of $40 000. At any time they wanted extra money, they could call the bank and on twenty-four hours' notice, could withdraw up to 80 per cent of their house's value, without any additional fees, or delay. This plan was particularly suitable for them, as Jim was self-employed and he put aside money each month to cover tax. By placing this money into their mortgage account, there were times throughout the year when they owed nothing.

Paying out a mortgage on the family home rates highly on my list of priorities. There is a wonderful sense of security knowing that you have a permanent home base, independent of the vagaries of the economy. It certainly adds to a feeling of prosperity.

If you have $20 000 owing on your mortgage and $20 000 invested in a bank account, you would be better off to pay out the mortgage, then borrow $20 000 to invest. The rationale for this is that you do not get any tax deduction for interest on a home mortgage, and you pay tax on the interest from your bank account. If you borrowed the money and then invested it, then the interest payments on the loan could be offset against the interest.

Before you race out and pay off your mortgage, check the position of your current loan. Shirley and her husband received an inheritance, and they decided to pay out their mortgage of $18 000 with some of the money. They had held the mortgage for a long time, so substantial amounts were now being deducted from the principal. The interest rate was about half market rates, and the repayments small. To continue paying the mortgage to full term would cost them $25 000. But if they invested this $18 000 into a capital guaranteed insurance bond for the same period, they would probably have around $40 000.

If they paid out the loan and saved the monthly repayments, the position would be different, but most people don't save.

The following table can be used to calculate how much you will save by paying out your mortgage early. An interest rate of 14 per cent has been assumed for all calculations.

Amount Borrowed	20 years	15 years	10 years	5 years	
$50 000	$622	$666	$777	$1163	Per month
$100 000	$1244	$1332	$1553	$2327	Per month
$150 000	$1866	$1998	$2330	$3490	Per month

Points to remember when shopping for credit:

Shop around, rates vary continually, ask what the interest rate is and if you are eligible for a preferred rate.

Check the real cost by multiplying the monthly amount by the term.

Check if insurance is included. If essential, it may be cheaper to arrange your own.

Ask if there is a penalty for early repayment, and what it is.

Never overcommit.
Ask if there is an interest-free period on charge or credit cards.

Lenders look for stability of address and employment and your capacity to repay a loan.

Appearances are important. Dress for success. Take along records to loan interview such as: bank books, investment certificates, salary slip, loan details.

Insurance—how much do you need?

Insurance companies sell on chance of disaster, and there are some people who have been sold insurance when it is not appropriate. For instance, single people without dependents rarely need life insurance, unless they particularly want to leave money to someone.

Mary asked me to check an insurance policy that had been sold to her. She was single, twenty-eight and had no superannuation. The policy was for $150 000 life cover, or, if Mary did not die before she was sixty she would receive this $150 000. In the early years most of her savings would go to pay for life cover, at a distant future date her life cover would decrease as savings grew. At this time in her life Mary had no need for life cover. If she invested the same amount into a superannuation policy she would receive approximately double the payout on maturity, as well as receive a tax deduction each year.

Lending institutions often stipulate that insurance be included on loans to protect them. But you do not have to take out insurance with the lender. Often shopping around for a better rate is more economical.

Income insurance pays a regular income if you are unable to work because of sickness or accident. But, most companies load premiums for women. In some cases, women pay double male rates. It is true that statistics prove women have more claims, but there are still some companies that offer the same rates for both men and women. Check around first.

Medical insurance is a purely individual decision. I rarely get sick so I do not feel that I need it, and have not had medical cover for years. Recently I had a lot of medical expenses, due to having a baby. The total cost to me, after refunds from Medicare for hospital, doctor and all tests, came to the same amount that I would have paid to a health fund for a year. And, I had my own specialist. If you feel you must have health cover, join a fund, but don't just do it because that is what you've always done.

Read all policies, don't just take the salesperson's word. It's not that they are dishonest, but they may be misinformed themselves. Make sure you are getting what you pay for.

Investing for profit

Are your savings and investments the best ones for today? Don't fall in love with your investments. Jean believed she was a conservative investor who was not prepared to take any chances, but half of her money was invested in mining shares that had been bought ten years ago. When I suggested that these shares were volatile and that she would be better off selling some she was horrified.

If your intention is to prosper from investments, sentiment plays no part. Investment cycles continually change and all investments should be reassessed using the criteria—are they profitable, or potentially profitable, today? If not, get rid of them.

Emotions can influence property owners as well. People have been known to keep rents low because they cannot face their tenants. It comes back to intentions. If you wish to give by keeping rents low, fine. If you are keeping rents below market level because you are not assertive, find a real estate agent to manage the property for you.

Ethical investments have grown in popularity over the past few years. An ethical investment is one that does not invest in tobacco companies, arms dealers or manufacturers, uranium miners, companies that pollute the atmosphere and so on. Many ethical investors have the mistaken belief that to support their cause they have to make less money. This is not so, as there are still many companies and investments available that give good returns and still meet ethical standards.

Investments to enjoy

There are people who are not motivated by investments, or by making money for money's sake. Alternatives that can be fun and still allow for profit do exist.

A *HOLIDAY HOME* is a perfect example. If the location is good and it's in reasonable condition, it can grow substantially in value as an asset, and provide family and friends with a wonderful retreat. If you rent it out when you're not using it, other people, not so fortunate, can benefit.

My uncle and his three adult sons bought a block of land near the sea a number of years ago. Later they built a kit home on it. They now have an investment that has grown considerably in value, which the whole extended family enjoys.

Build a *TRAVEL ACCOUNT*. Insurance bonds are the ideal investment for this goal. Lisa puts $80 a month into an insurance bond, and she intends increasing her savings each year in line with inflation. In ten years' time she could have around $25 000. This fund will then finance her future holidays. The reason she chose an insurance bond for this purpose is that all savings are tax free after ten years. Lisa also has the option to draw on this account at any time if her circumstances change. Insurance bonds may be invested in by either lump sum or by regular savings.

Think of investments as lifestyle, rather than as just dollars sitting in the bank.

COLLECTORS can make handsome profits from hobbies, and you don't necessarily need to buy expensive works of art. Comics have emerged as an investment alternative in the United States and is following suit in Australia. When I was a child, my sister and I were avid readers of *The Phantom*. After a while we would throw them out, swap with friends or take them to the book exchange. A copy that was worth pennies to us then can be sold for $1000 today. Even comic strips from Sunday papers have been sold for high prices.

Stamp, coins and vintage cars have been around for years as collectors' items, but there is always a niche for something different. As you clean out your cupboards, look to see if there is anything that could be valuable now, or in years to come. My brother-in-law was about to throw out my mother's old sewing machine stand, which I salvaged because I liked it. I was told recently they now sell for $300 and who knows what it may be worth in years to come? Licence plates on cars, even old wireless sets now have a high value.

Antiques are also collectors' items which can give pleasure and be functional pieces of furniture as well. Rare books can provide pleasure and profit, and good wine always increases in value with age. Use your imagination and prosper from a hobby.

WORKS OF ART

Collectors come in all shapes and sizes, and buy for all types of reasons. There are those who want to decorate their houses; those who want the prestige of owning an original; or those that collect for profit. Others buy for the sheer joy of it.

Amazingly, throughout periods of recession, or the stock market crash, prices of artworks have not been affected, and many pieces have seen tremendous gains in value over the past twenty-odd years. But prices can be manipulated by unscrupulous dealers, just like any other business. At auctions, reserves can be inflated, to create the impression of a greater value. At exhibitions, sold stickers can be placed on pieces, to give the impression of a greater demand.

Many of the longer-established galleries are the most respected, and have attracted corporate investors. Art collection is a long-term investment and you should not be rushed into a decision. Talk to galleries. Dealers want ongoing customers, so they will be more than happy to advise you and read as many articles on the subject as you can. A mid-range investor is one who spends about $250 000. We don't all have that much, but good works of art can be bought for a few thousand dollars. Beware of galleries that guarantee to buy artworks back at a set price in the future. They may not be around that long.

Superannuation—do you know enough?

Superannuation is money set aside for retirement. Years ago, employers offered this opportunity to staff and most would join without giving any consideration to the details of the fund.

All superannuation funds are not the same. Some can fluctuate in value, others guarantee to pay a multiple of the employee's final salary. Some pay a pension, some pay a lump sum. In some, the employer pays all the contributions; with others, both employer and employee contribute.

Some investors mistakenly believe that if they place their money with a bank it is automatically safe. This is not necessarily so.

Herman migrated to Australia after the war, and by scrimping and saving all his life, managed to save $100 000. Following the advice of a bank employee, he placed a fair amount of this money with the bank's superannuation fund. What the bank employee neglected to tell him was that the investment was unit linked, meaning that it could go down as well as up in value. Like many people, Herman did not read his policy document. The stockmarket crashed and at 67, when he should have been looking forward to a comfortable retirement,Herman lost $30 000.

Nowadays very few people stay with the one employer for a long time. Check if your company's superannuation fund is worthwhile, if you leave in a few years. These questions are not easily answered, as conditions differ from company to company. Ask for written information, ask questions, and if in doubt, seek an opinion from a financial adviser.

If you join a personal fund, always check out the fees. In a recent survey I undertook of private superannuation funds with insurance companies, there was a variation of $200 000 in the payout figure between the best and the worst company. And that was assuming that contributions, interest rates and all factors were equal.

Are you paying too much tax?

Before investing in joint names, or in the name of the highest income earner alone, consider your tax position.

John earns $36 000 while his wife Hazel does not work. They invested their life savings of $100 000 in a bank account paying 11.5 per cent interest in joint names. Combined tax for John and Hazel totalled $3100. If they had placed this money in Hazel's name, tax could have been reduced to $1536, saving $1564 a year.

If John and Hazel invested their money in a high growth property trust, earning the same rate of interest, their savings could grow to considerably more over the same period. The reason for this is that they do not pay tax until investment is withdrawn, and this would be at a reduced rate because capital gains tax would apply. Using a tax-advantaged investment would probably give them around $70 000 more, over ten years.

Tax-advantaged investments are there to be used when appropriate. If you need income from investments to live on, then invest in term deposits, mortgages, shares that pay a franked dividend, debentures, bank bills and so on. If you don't need the income, reduce tax by investing for growth in insurance bonds, friendly society bonds, property, shares or collectables.

Investing for growth means that the value of the investment grows, but you don't receive this profit until you sell. Much like the family home, what it is worth today is considerably more than what it was worth ten years ago. This gain in value is called capital growth.

Capital gains tax may apply to some of these investments but is not payable until investment is cashed in or sold. Because an allowance is built into capital gains tax for inflation, the tax is reduced. In some cases, where insurance and friendly society bonds are used, there would be no tax.

Tax is paid on a scale, so the more you earn, the more tax you pay. If you do not know your marginal tax rate (the last tax bracket you were in), ask your employer, or call your local Taxation office. There is no need to go into personal details. As long as you tell them your annual income, they can tell you what your marginal tax rate is. The 1988–89 tax rates are:

0–$5100	Nil tax
$5101–$17 650	21 per cent
$17 651–$20 600	29 per cent
$20 601–$35 000	39 per cent
$35 001–50 000	47 per cent
over $50 001	49 per cent

Provisional tax applies to income other than your salary which exceeds $1000 a year. This assumes that your salary has had P.A.Y.E. (pay as you earn) tax deducted. If you are self-employed you may also have to pay provisional tax.

If you are an ordinary taxpayer and your additional income is more than $999 and less than $8000 for the year, you will have to pay tax on this year's income, plus tax on next year's, by 31 March. Next year's income will be assessed as being 10 per cent higher, so your provisional tax for next year will be slightly more.

If you earn more than $5000 a year from other sources, then provisional tax would be payable quarterly.

There may be times when this extra income is only a temporary thing. For instance, you may sell your home and have an amount invested for a few months only. In cases such as this, you can apply to the Taxation Department to have this provisional tax reassessed.

Points to Remember:

* Ensure that you are not paying too much tax if investing in joint names. Tax applies on a sliding scale; the more you earn the more you pay.
* Be cautious about placing investments in children's names to avoid tax. Children can earn $416 a year

tax free, after which they pay a very high tax rate.
* Investments placed in trust for children still have to be declared on the trustees tax return, and tax paid.
* Leave money readily available for opportunities or unexpected expenses and invest the balance into capital growth investments.

CHAPTER 11

Financial personalities

She said 'I just can't stand it any more. Since the stock-market crash I've done nothing but think about money. I suppose I was very naive, but it never occurred to me that anything could happen. I don't want to live this way. I just want to invest, knowing that my money is safe, so that I can forget about it'.

There is no single investment strategy to suit everyone. Financial personalities are as individual as you are. They are not cast in concrete, and deciding which category you fit into is merely an indicator of your comfort level. If you try to change too quickly you'll find your decisions hard to live with.

Some people are prepared to take risks and accept losses. Others want the profits, but are not prepared to take any losses. It is all a matter of choice.

In May 1962 the American stock-market fell and newspaper headlines quoted 'Black Monday Panic on Wall Street . . . Nation Fears New 1929 Debacle'. In October 1987 the American stock-market crashed again, and headlines called it 'Black Monday' again. For months there was talk that this crash was a repeat of the 1929 Wall Street crash.

The general population, led by the media because bad news sells, focuses its attention on fear and loss. As mentioned in an earlier chapter, what you focus on you generally get. Take precautions by all means, but use your own judgement and seek advice, apply it to your own situation and don't be swayed by the masses. The masses are not rich.

J. Paul Getty, one of the world's richest men, began buying stocks at the depth of the Depression. Most people were too fearful. Twenty to thirty years later some of those stocks were worth one hundred times what he paid for them. There are other similar success stories.

Each and every one of us decides our own level of prosperity, not the economy. People who are debt-free and cashed up when a recession comes are usually in a perfect position to prosper.

On the other hand, if you have lost money, take immediate steps to remedy the situation. Complaining to all and sundry doesn't improve anything. The fact that you are putting so much energy into your adversity will only make it worse.

There are no get-rich-quick schemes that last. The road to riches is paved with opportunities and opportunists. Sometimes you will be side-tracked. Sometimes you will make errors in judgement. As long as your focus remains on the ultimate goal and you remain positive, you cannot help but achieve what you want.

Decide what type of investor you are, and what level of risk you are prepared to take. A conservative investor can still accumulate wealth.

During your period of acquiring knowledge and building up an investment account, you may not be prepared to take any risks and that's a good idea. A setback at this time may stop you from trying again. Once you are established and feeling more confident, you can diversify, even speculate, with a proportion of your capital.

Start where you feel comfortable now, and don't let yourself be swayed by anyone. We all have different values, so what is right for your partner may not be right for you.

If you are married or in a partnership I suggest you discuss your comfort level with your partner, in order to avoid conflict later on.

The passive investor

There are passive and active investors. A passive investor could be someone who doesn't have the time to manage an investment portfolio, or doesn't want to be bothered with all the details, or someone who may simply not have sufficient money to do otherwise.

Many people presume that I am an active investor, because I work in the industry. After advising other people all day, the last thing I want to do in my leisure time is watch my investments, so I prefer to leave it to the experts. For people like me, unit trusts and bonds are the answer. They are ideal for anyone starting out, as you can start your investment portfolio with only $1000, or monthly savings of $100.

Fund managers have the best research to closely monitor trends, and are often specialists in their individual fields. By investing in unit trusts you can be part-owner of shares in Australian or overseas companies, property, rural property, tourist resorts, gold, futures contracts, and any number of options. There are always new products coming onto the market.

Expert advice is essential to select the funds suitable for you. Don't just believe everything the advertisements say, as that's often clever marketing. Make sure that the fund managers have a good track record.

A passive investor can also borrow to invest. If investing in a property trust the added benefits are: less capital needed, no maintenance costs, no problems with tenants, no legal fees or stamp duty costs, your investment is readily cashable when you want your money back, no need to wait for a buyer, and no agents' fees.

A passive investor can be conservative or flamboyant and there are managed investments to suit all types of personalities. When the stock-market was riding high, quite a few of my clients made over 100 per cent in a year by investing in Japanese shares, and they all took their profits long before the crash.

Being passive does not mean that you hand responsibility for your affairs over to someone else entirely. Actress Doris Day handed millions over to her husband to invest. He in turn handed them over to another adviser. They lost the lot and it was not until her husband died that she discovered that she had no money.

A passive investor may change with different life cycles. There may come a time when you have more time and more money and you prefer to become directly involved. Passive investing is a good place for beginners to start. As you read investment reports and follow your investment, you will gain knowledge you may wish to use at some future date.

Investments to Suit Passive Investors: Bank/Building Society/Credit Union Accounts. All unit trusts, insurance bonds, friendly society bonds, term deposits, debentures, government bonds, bank bills, cash management trusts.

The active investor

An active investor is one who likes to remain in control. This type of person would be happier with direct investments in property and shares. If you are going to be an active investor you must have some knowledge of the market and investment cycles. Investment objectives must be clear: is the investment to reduce tax, provide income or capital growth? Active investors still need expert advice, particularly in regard to gearing, taxation and share purchases.

An active investor can be a speculator or conservative. Often it's wisest to specialise in one area such as property or shares. By buying with the intention of holding onto property for long periods, there is less need to worry about investment cycles as time is on your side.

Julie was bored in her job and often she would sit with nothing to do. She started reading the financial papers and became familiar with public companies, and the people running them. Julie decided to invest just a little, starting with a thousand dollars. As her knowledge grew, and she made some profits, so did her share portfolio. Although her salary was low, she made enough money to buy a home in one of the best areas of Sydney, and still have money left over. To Julie, investing was a very profitable hobby.

To be an active investor, you need time and cash flow. Property owners need to allow for periods when property is untenanted and for maintenance costs. A share trader needs to keep some cash available for unexpected opportunities.

Investments to Suit Active Investors: Property, shares, options, gold, futures, collectables.

The conservative investor

A conservative investor is very security conscious and doesn't like taking any risks at all. This type of investor would leave money in low interest savings bank account, or put all the money into fixed interest investments and often pay more tax than necessary. Being security conscious doesn't mean you have no choices and there are ways to invest securely and reduce tax.

The danger for security conscious investors is that they are so concerned about losing money, they do nothing at all.

'I'll do whatever you say' she said. She had $300 000 in the bank, and did not want to pay too much tax. As she preferred property investments, I suggested she buy a property, but borrow just enough to cover the rent that she would receive. She could then invest the balance into capital guaranteed insurance bonds. This way she would pay no tax, and have an investment of $350 000 growing for her, because she geared her investment. In the event of a major catastrophe she could easily pay out the loan with the money she had invested in bonds.

She agreed, she would do it. Two months later she said she would do it. Six months later she is still saying it. Unfortunately, because of her inability to make a decision, she should be up for a tax bill of $23 000 this year, plus another $25 000 for provisional tax.

Margaret was very security conscious. She received a superannuation pension of $15 000 a year from her former employer. She also had $200 000 invested with the bank. Her annual income was greater than she needed and she was paying $12 000 a year tax, but Margaret believed that only banks have safe investments.

A more tax-efficient alternative for Margaret would be to invest sufficient of her capital with the bank, to give her the extra income that she required. She estimated that she needed $19 000 a year after tax. The rest of her money could be invested in a secure capital growth type investment such as, capital guaranteed insurance bonds. She would still have security but would save about $6000 a year in tax. If Margaret invested this $6000 for ten years at 10 per cent, she would have another $90 000 to spend on herself, or leave to her children. As it is, only the Taxation Department and the bank benefit from her plan.

Having worked in a bank, I know that there are thousands of people literally throwing away money every year. It's natural that older people, particularly those who lived through the Depression, feel fearful. When they were young there just weren't the range of investments that there are today, and it can all seem a bit overwhelming. Often such people have worked hard for their money, have never sought advice in the past, and they don't know who to trust today.

If you have a substantial amount of money, then advice is essential. You can read through the check-list in a later section of this book on how to choose an adviser, but beyond that, trust your own judgement. Intuition often tells us who to trust and who not to. Just make sure that it is not fear dictating your actions.

Age has nothing to do with being security conscious and slow and steady can still make a lot of money. But if you would like to be a little more adventurous, invest just a small amount, say 10 per cent of your savings, into something like shares. If you make a profit, sell half and put it back with your safe investments. Don't just rush into buying something like shares because you've finally decided to take the plunge. Timing is important, so again you will need professional advice. Some people decide it's time to take chances right now and take no notice of market conditions.

Make sure that any investment that sounds safe really is. Some investments have names that are misleading. One bank had a product called 'supersafe'. Despite the name, it was a unit linked investment, meaning that it could fluctuate in value. When the share-market crashed, it fell in value. Ask if your investment can fluctuate in value. If it is called guaranteed, ask how secure the guarantee is, and what it is backed by.

Investments to Suit Conservative Investors: Bank and Building Society Accounts; Government Bonds; Semi-Government Loans, e.g., Waterboard, Telecom Loans; Property, providing it is bought for the long-term; Bank Bills; Cash Management Trusts; Capital Guaranteed Insurance Bonds; Friendly Society Bonds; Capital Guaranteed Annuities; Capital Guaranteed Superannuation; Debentures.

The average investor

The average investor lies somewhere between the conservative investor and the flamboyant personality. This investor could invest in shares or property, as long as they were considered long term investments. This person would enjoy investments that are functional as well as profitable such as a holiday home or a work of art.

Average investors often make the most profits because they are prepared to take some risks, but do not gamble. Investments taken out for the long-term are not affected by market cycles as severely. Long-term, most investments will come out well.

She opened her handbag and rummaged for her investment certificates, 'I don't have very much, just the money I've saved all our life, but we seem to be paying an awful lot of tax'. Mavis was in her late seventies, and a bit forgetful. An awful lot of tax turned out to be $60 000 a year, a lot of tax to anyone. Her little bit of money totalled just under $400 000 in investments, plus a small block of units.

Mavis and her husband lived through the Depression and made a decision to save, so that they would never have to struggle again. Mavis's husband had worked as a salesman, so his salary was only average. Each time they saved money, they bought another unit, or some shares. Over a working life they managed to acquire just under a million dollars in assets.

Investments to Suit Average Investors: Shares; Property; Unit Trusts; Insurance Bonds; Friendly Society Bonds; Government Bonds; Semi-Government Loans; Debentures; Mortgages; Cash Management Trusts; Paintings; Collectables; Shares.

The flamboyant investor

Usually investors prepared to take big risks are after big gains. Many successful entrepreneurs fit into this category, but they are not foolish either. There are calculated risks, and just plain gambles.

People who decide they want to make BIG MONEY, are often in a hurry to do so. Consequently, they are more likely to jump into the first get-rich-quick scheme that comes along. This is self-sabotage.

One example of such a scheme was a certain type of leveraged currency scheme popular a couple of years back. The companies involved were not members of any recognised futures exchange. Salespeople would ring people at random, or in response to a coupon sent in from an advertisement. The lure was big profits from foreign currency transactions. The investor only had to invest a portion of the investment, say $10 000, but $100 000 would be invested on their behalf.

Two of these salespeople were known to me. They worked on a commission basis and made up to $250 000 a year each. They were just salespeople, whose previous experience was door-to-door selling, or used cars. They had no experience in the industry, and no great knowledge. Gullible investors, on the strength of a phone call, would invest amounts up to $100 000, based on the advice of these dubious advisers. These same salespeople told me they would never consider investing their own money.

Eventually many of these companies could not return money to their investors, and after much media coverage, were closed down. Hundreds of investors lost money. Not all futures funds are bad. There are some that offer opportunities for large profits with limited risk. Make sure you deal with a recognised company.

To make a lot of money in a short period of time you need to use other people's money. This is commonly referred to as gearing. If you invest $10 000, you only earn interest on $10 000. If you invest $10 000 of your own money, but borrow another $90 000, you have a much larger sum working for you.

Gearing for property purchases is common, but investors can borrow to invest in shares, unit trusts, and so on. Make it a rule never to overcommit. The family home is often used as security for a loan. Use this asset if you wish, but never borrow any more than you can repay if the venture fails. If you follow this rule, you may have temporary setbacks, but you will never suffer a major financial catastrophe.

Once you've made a profit, pay out the mortgage and speculate with what is left. You can always borrow more by using your investments as security.

Timing is vitally important, more so for the flamboyant investor. Make allowance for temporary downturns. Balance your portfolio with some more secure investments as well. Set contingency plans, and always keep some cash in reserve, so that you can act when opportunities come.

Investments to Suit Flamboyant Investors: Property; Shares; Options; Futures; Gold; most Unit Linked Trusts e.g., International Shares, special situations funds.

CHAPTER 12

Accumulating wealth

Can an ordinary person, on an ordinary wage, become wealthy? The answer is yes, as long as you believe you can.

A common belief is that wealth can only be acquired by luck, inheritance or entrepreneurial skill. If time is on your side, then wealth is easily within your reach, provided that you are prepared to save and invest regularly.

An average wage earner can earn over a million dollars during a normal working life. How much of it will you have saved?

The main reason people don't save is that there is not enough left over. If you want to leave behind the belief that there is never enough, you should begin by paying yourself an allowance out of each pay. It may take a while to rearrange your affairs to a level where you can save 10 per cent of income, but the incentives are high. Once you see your money growing, you will be motivated.

Save regularly now, no matter how little. Open a 'wealth account' and use it for no other purpose than to build a base for future investments. This in turn will achieve your major long-term goals. Saving is vitally important, not only for you personally, as it does help to make you feel secure and prosperous, but it assists our economy as well.

Nations such as Japan are big savers, and their inflation rate is one of the lowest in the world, and their economy is healthy. In the last decade Australia's level of savings has declined, and our economic problems have increased. People who save help both the economy and themselves.

Enjoy your money. Don't think of investments as a pile of money growing, unless that is what motivates you. Think of it instead in terms of lifestyle, a holiday home, a travel fund, a red Ferrari, or a home by the sea.

If you want to make money, or keep the money that you have, you need to know something about investment cycles and you need expert advice. Inflation and taxation will quickly eat up your capital, and bad advice will get rid of it even faster.

The power of compound interest

Compound interest gives you interest on your interest. Invest $1000 at 10 per cent, and you have $1100. Leave this interest in your account and next year you earn interest on $1100 and so it increases each year. Regular savings, where capital and interest are left to compound, can grow to some staggering amounts. For example, if you save $46 a week ($200 a month) and leave it to compound at an average return of 11 per cent per annum, your money would grow to the following amounts:

$15 902	$43 399	$173 127	$1 720 024
5yrs	10yrs	20yrs	40yrs

These estimates do not allow for tax or inflation. Inflation will naturally take its toll, but you can counteract this by increasing savings each year in line with salary rises. By saving regularly over a long period you can become a multi-millionaire, and this applies to even a conservative investor who doesn't want to take any risks.

Save 10 per cent

Develop the habit of saving 10 per cent of everything you earn and you will always have plenty. Don't just put it all in a bank account. Make your money work for you by using investments that have tax advantages such as insurance bonds, property, shares or superannuation.

A difference of just 3 per cent in the earning rate of your investment does not make a huge difference in a short period, but take it over a long term and the amount almost doubles.

Save $67 a week @ 10 per cent for 30 years $656 287	Save $67 a week @ 13 per cent for 30 years $1 269 701

The Rule of 72

By dividing any number into 72 you can find the approximate number of years it takes to double your money. If you want to double your money in five years divide 5 into 72, and you know that your investment needs to earn 14.4 per cent per annum, for you to reach your target. There will be times when you need this knowledge, when buying a home, planning for retirement or planning a world trip.

The doubling effect of money can be quite amazing. $10 000 growing to $20 000 over five years is not so unusual, but the same initial investment over twenty years would have grown to $160 000. This is why superannuation funds grow so rapidly in the last ten years of your working life. Retire at age sixty and you may be entitled to $500 000, but wait five more years and retire at age sixty-five, and you could be entitled to $1 000 000.

Negative gearing

Borrowing to invest is called gearing. When the loan repayments exceed the income earned by the investment, it is called negative gearing. There are tax benefits to negative gearing. Losses incurred can be deducted from your normal income, thereby reducing your overall tax. The other advantage is a greater return on your investment because you have a much larger amount invested, but there are risks involved.

You must have sufficient cash flow to make up the difference between the income you receive from investment and the loan repayments. Although you will receive a tax refund, this only comes in once a year, after you have already paid out the money. If your investment is in property, you also need funds to cover rates and maintenance, and to allow for any periods the property is not rented.

To be eligible for a tax deduction for gearing, you must earn income from an investment, so land, insurance bonds or friendly society bonds are not suitable. Shares, property, even term deposits are all suitable. You can own the investments yourself or invest in a trust.

If negative gearing to purchase shares, then you need to be extra cautious, because a sudden drop in share prices will dramatically reduce the value of your investment. You still have to pay out the loan even if you lose all your money.

Julie and her sister decided to buy a holiday unit, and they had $26 000 between them. They borrowed $80 000 and used $20 000 as a deposit. They have no intention of selling this unit in the future, so they took out a loan where principal and interest would be repaid over fifteen years. The interest component of this loan would be tax deductible. In order to calculate the cost to them, we made the following assumptions:

Income—property would be let half the year and over Christmas holidays, say		$6000
Less	Agents commission	($ 700)
	Cleaning expenses	($1000)
	Rates	($ 600)
	Strata Levy	($ 300)
	Provision for Maintenance	($1000)
	Loan repayments ($1120 per month)	($13 440)
	Loss	($11 040)

This loss is divided between Julie and her sister equally, so they both have a loss of $5520 to deduct from their regular income on their tax return. Tax rates are constantly changing, so I have included tax scales in another section of this book. Using the tax rate applying at the time of writing, 49 per cent, Julie and her sister should each receive a tax refund of $2670. When you take this off the amount they have had to outlay, the real cost to each of them has been $55 a week. Considering that they have a property valued at $100 000 which should grow in value by about 10–12 per cent a year, this is an excellent investment.

With each passing year, this tax position will alter. Rents will rise and the interest on the loan will reduce as more payments are made, so a regular yearly review is essential. Julie hopes to buy another property as the equity in the first property increases.

Many people use negative gearing for property purchases. It is likely to continue to be a viable investment for some time. Not so long ago, the Tax Department decided to scrap tax deductions for negative gearing and consequently a lot of investors stopped buying property. Property prices slumped and and rents skyrocketed, and there was a rental crisis, because there were fewer properties available. Tax deductions for negative gearing were restored. Therefore, allowing tax deductions for this type of investment follows very much the double win principle. The tax laws don't just favour the wealthy, as some people mistakenly believe.

To invest in property you will need a deposit of around 20 per cent, but this could change when loans are harder to obtain. For shares you will need a large portion of your own money—possibly 30–40 per cent. If your income is large enough to cover the loan repayments, as well as normal living expenses, you should be able to get a loan. The property or shares are held as security by the lender. Ideally most of the income received from the investment will pay off the loan, with very little effort on your part.

It is easy to get excited at the prospect of multiplying your money quickly. Sidestep the pitfalls by ensuring that:

* You can cover loan repayments without income from investment.
* You have funds available for maintenance, rates, strata levy, lawn mowing.
* You have sufficient capital to cover yourself during any downturn in the market.
* Just because the markets are riding high, never, never, never buy rubbish. You will live to regret it. There are good and bad buys, so search for quality.
* Learn the importance of timing and try not to buy at the top of the market.
* Never overcommit.
* Always have a contingency plan.

Allow for inflation

Inflation can work for or against you. If you have borrowed money to invest, and have a large sum working for you, then inflation can work for you. Take Julie and her sister for example. They have a home unit that cost them $100 000 to buy. If they keep this home unit for fifteen years until the loan is paid out, their investment could have grown to $417 700. That's assuming that their unit averages 10 per cent per annum capital growth. That's still way ahead of inflation. At first it cost them $55 a week, but as time goes by and rents increase, it would cost them nothing. What many people do at this time, is buy another property, so that you are continually adding to your investment portfolio.

If you are in debt, or find it difficult to save, then inflation works against you, with prices skyrocketing each year. It is never too late to get started, so save towards that initial deposit now, or find someone to invest with you. When you have a prosperity consciousness, you work with the conditions that surround you, not moan about how hard it is to get started. Once you take the first steps, even when your goal seems impossible to achieve, then opportunities often come along to assist you.

The chart below shows the value of $10 000, allowing for different rates of inflation.

INFLATION RATE	VALUE IN 20 years	VALUE IN 10 years	VALUE IN 5 years
5%	$3769	$6139	$7835
6%	$3118	$5584	$7473
7%	$2584	$3624	$7130

Investment cycles

Because of the cyclical nature of investments, there are times when it is advantageous to lock into high interest rates, or to buy and sell shares and property. Investment cycles cannot be guaranteed, as they can be affected by the government's monetary policy and world events. Assumptions for future trends are mostly based on what has happened in the past, and there are always exceptions. If you look at graphs of investments over the last eighty years, you will see that the same patterns emerge time after time. By following these cycles and using your own intuition, you will get it right most of the time. This investment clock can be used as a guide to assess general trends for investments.

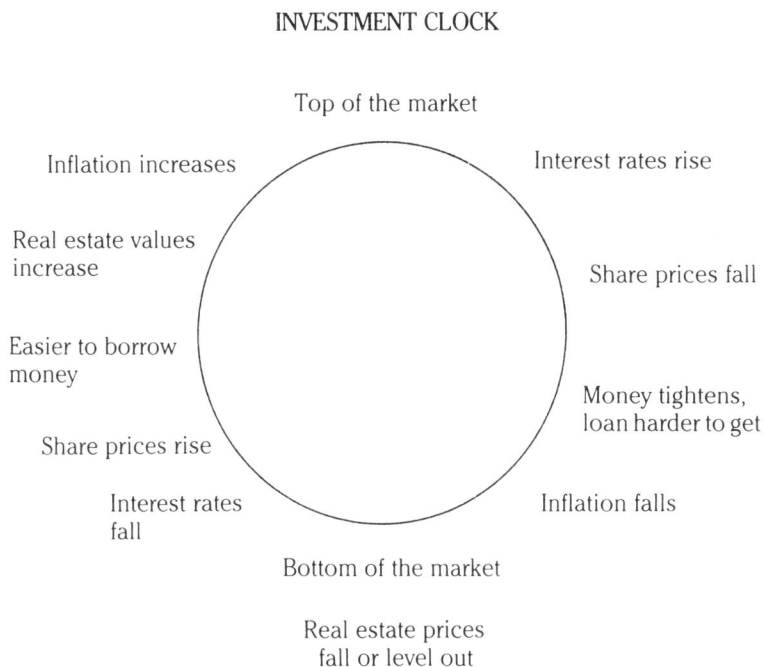

INVESTMENT CLOCK

Top of the market

Inflation increases

Interest rates rise

Real estate values increase

Share prices fall

Easier to borrow money

Money tightens, loan harder to get

Share prices rise

Interest rates fall

Inflation falls

Bottom of the market

Real estate prices fall or level out

Where to go for advice

Learning what to look for and where to go for advice can be an awesome task. If you remember the example of how just 3 per cent difference in the interest rate nearly doubled the value of the investment over a long period, you'll understand how vital good advice is.

A financial adviser will give recommendations on specific investments, but many do more than this. Some advisers cover budgeting, personal insurance, superannuation, taxation and pensions. Ensure that the person giving the advice is qualified. It is preferable to have an independent adviser, as agents acting for individual companies can only recommend their products. The following list details some of the types of advisers and the services they provide. It is by no means comprehensive and will vary with the individual firm.

Investment/Financial Advisers, or licensed dealers' representatives, as their consultants are called, usually cover the whole spectrum of financial planning and can assist you with advice on pensions, taxation, retirement planning as well as investments, insurance and superannuation.

Stockbrokers: In addition to advising on the buying and selling of shares, many brokers now offer other financial services similar to investment advisers. Some firms deal mainly with corporate clients, so check with your local Stock Exchange advisory service as to which firms can help you.

My experience has been that stockbrokers are very interested in financial planning clients when the share market is depressed. During boom times it is hard to get any service, unless you are a major investor.

Accountants: Many accounting firms are now offering financial planning advice, but ensure that they have access to adequate research. Investment advice is a full-time profession, and while there are accountants who may be excellent in this area, my opinion is that they don't always have the time after keeping up with taxation changes to know everything about investment management as well.

Banks/Building Societies/Credit Unions: Some offer full financial planning services. Some will be biased towards their own products, others will not. Use your own judgement.

Most advisers make their money from commissions paid by investment companies. Investors do not save money by dealing directly with the investment company, so it is still worthwhile seeking independent professional advice.

There will always be some advisers who will recommend products because of the high commission they pay, but there are still many others who will not. It is your money and you are entitled to the best possible advice. If in doubt, have a plan done and have it checked by your accountant and always ask questions.

Advisory firms charge a fee for their time, but this can be refunded to you if they earn commission. Stockbrokers charge a percentage of the value of the shares, each time you buy and sell.

When seeking an adviser you can contact a professional association and ask for a recommendation. There are two associations, the Australian Investment Planners Association (A.I.P.A.) and the International Association for Financial Planning (I.A.F.P.). Both should be listed in the phone book in all major cities. Ask them for a member firm in your area.

You could select someone from an advertisement, but the best recommendations are always from someone who has been to them. There is no need to worry about confidentiality, as a good adviser will never discuss your situation with a friend or family member. A number of advisers hold free seminars in order to attract new business. You can ask for your name to be placed on the mailing list.

Check carefully the advice that is given to you and always ask questions. A client of mine brought along a plan that had been prepared by another organisation. In this plan was a recommendation for an investment in a fairly speculative share trust. That's O.K., as long as the client is aware of this. The comments about this trust read 'This company has public trustee status, therefore, all have *guaranteed* buy back agreements in the Trust Deed'. My client naturally interpreted this to be a safe investment, which it was not. The buy back guarantee only means that the company will buy back your units, at current market value, which may only be worth half the value of the original purchase.

Another organisation promotes itself under the guise of education. Its main activity is selling insurance products, most of which have high charges.

If you are really interested in learning more, investigate what courses are available. The Securities Institute runs a number of courses. You can do individual subjects, such as basic economics or financial planning, or complete the whole Certificate course. As this course is very popular, it is sometimes difficult to get in and preference is given to those who work in the industry. Stock Exchanges often run introductory courses. Ring your local Exchange to find out what is available. Some investment advisers run courses, as well as evening colleges, T.A.F.E., or W.E.A.

Contacting an adviser

When I sold one of my businesses it was the first time in my life that I had a substantial sum, and I didn't know what to do with it or where to go for advice. At that time there was not the plethora of advisers that there are today, and no magazines for the lay person. So I paid off some debts, went on a holiday, and over time managed to fritter the rest away. Knowing what I know now, I could have trebled that money, but I didn't know.

So how do you make that initial contact? Obviously if you have a recommendation it's easier, as you have some idea of what service the firm provides. If not, take courage and ring and ask. The first thing to do is to say how much you have to invest, and ask if they give advice to people with such an amount. I'm presuming here that the sum is small. If you have $50 000 or more, any adviser would love to see you. If you don't have any money to invest, but need advice on how to get started, tell them. Some advisers aren't interested, so you haven't wasted their time or yours. Others charge a higher fee for such advice, to cover their time. Spending a hundred or two now could save you thousands later on.

If you decide to make an appointment, ask to speak to the consultant that you'll be seeing. Establishing rapport, is important. If you don't like the person on the phone, chances are you won't at the interview, and you may be wasting your time. Some advisers are patronising, which you don't have to put up with, while others you simply may not click with. Ask what information to bring with you, as this can save you time and money. It is difficult giving advice to someone who doesn't know how much they earn, how much money they have, or how much they need to live on. We can't work miracles.

Think about your goals, short and long-term. Your adviser will want to know a lot about you, and what you want from life. It is not an invasion of privacy. Information like this is vital to prepare the best plan for you.

Questions to ask: Is the firm well-established, and can consultants advise on all types of investments?

Is the adviser licensed?

What is the adviser's background/experience?

Is a fee charged and if so, is it refundable if you place your investments through the firm?

Ask for investment advice in writing. Don't invest on the first visit, unless you are absolutely confident, and make sure that you feel comfortable with the person giving advice.

CHAPTER 13

Planning for everyone

Children

Having my eldest and youngest child nineteen years apart has been a great opportunity for me to plan for two entirely different situations. When Lisa was young, there just wasn't the money to save for her; nor would I have known what to do with it anyway. What I have been able to give her is good advice, so that now she is working, she can make her own money work for her.

Laura has come along at a time when I have a great deal more knowledge and more money, so I'd like to make life easier for her, but at the same time teach her to be responsible with money.

Laura, although only a baby, gets pocket money of $2 each week. By the time she is five, and possibly wants to have some of this money, she will have $500 in the bank. My aim is to help her develop a prosperity consciousness at an early age by always having money of her own. She will be able to draw on this money for presents, or something extraordinary, but not just to spend or buy toys. Out of future pocket money, she will always have to save 10 per cent.

As well as this, I contribute to a savings plan on her behalf. Saving $20 a week, and increasing the savings each year with inflation, means that Laura could have $100 000 when she turns twenty-one. In real terms, allowing for inflation again, that will probably be worth about $25 000 today, a nice start. I've planned it so that the policy matures a few days before her twenty-first, but if I feel that she is not responsible enough to have that money then, I can withdraw the money prior to maturity.

Encourage children to manage their own money at an early age. When we went on holiday when my children were younger, they were allocated an amount of money for the week. This money was to buy ice creams, pay for rides, pictures, whatever they wanted. Once it ran out, they got no more. It's uncanny to see a child who happily spends all your money, turn into a real scrooge when it's theirs.

Spending and saving habits are developed at an early age. If you never encourage your children to be responsible with small amounts, it's unlikely that they will suddenly change when they start work. Foster a prosperity con-sciousness by teaching responsibility, rather than saying 'we can't afford it'. Children model themselves on your actions rather than your words, so give them something positive to emulate.

Singles—under thirty

It took a few attempts at budgeting and saving to find a plan that worked for Lisa, but persistence paid off. Like many young people, Lisa hates being restricted by a budget. She likes to travel overseas once a year, loves clothes and wants a car of her own. She has already learnt the hard way about overspending on credit cards, and now wants to live debt-free but still have money to enjoy herself and plan for the future.

Lisa's major asset is her expectation of being rich and she constantly attracts opportunities and money. At age twenty, she has a net income of $350 a week. Board and living costs amount to $100 a week, superannuation totals another $18 a week, and an insurance bond savings plan takes another $18 a week. This leaves her with $214 to save or spend as she pleases.

Lisa joined a superannuation fund now, so that she can stop contributing later on when she has the expense of a mortgage. Her superannuation savings will still work for her. Her insurance bond savings is for her travel account, and she should have $25 000 in ten years, provided she increases her savings each year to allow for inflation. Both lots of savings are automatically deducted from her bank account, making saving easy for her. The less effort it takes, the more likely you are to succeed.

Lisa is now saving for a deposit on a home unit. She hopes a friend will join with her and negative gear this property. They will need a deposit of $20 000 between them, so if they save $100 a week for the next two years, they should be able to achieve this target. The rent from the unit will repay most of the loan, but they may have to continue putting in $50 a week to cover expenses. This will only be for a couple of years, and each year Lisa's salary will increase.

Other opportunities may present themselves, so Lisa still has the ability to change direction without loss. Meanwhile she has the security of knowing that she will have a sound financial base on which to build.

This is the easiest time in anyone's life to build up capital, particularly while living at home. If money is managed efficiently, there should still enough for overseas trips and fun, while assets are being acquired.

It is also the ideal time to join a superannuation fund, as superannuation savings can cease once you buy a home. For instance, saving $100 a month into superannuation over five years amounts to $6000. If this is a portable fund, then you receive a tax deduction, which for an average salary earner would total $2400 over the five years. So in reality, savings only amounted to $3600.

After the initial five years, if no more was put into this fund, and it was left to earn interest for the next thirty years at 13 per cent, it would grow to $311 667. This would only apply to a superannuation fund with low charges, say 5 per cent of each contribution. A fund that takes a large percentage of what you pay in for the first few years would not do so well.

Singles—over thirty

If I had known years ago, what I know now, I could have been much better off financially. Unfortunately most of us didn't have the knowledge. So if you are over thirty, don't despair. Forget about finding a rich husband or inheriting money. Both could be a lovely bonus, but cannot be relied upon to come your way.

Carol was thirty-two and had a few thousand in savings. Her annual salary was $36 000. She wanted to buy a home unit and provide financial security for her later years. She was able to allocate $600 a month towards these goals.

From this amount we set aside $100 a month for superannuation. As Carol is taking out a personal superannuation policy, this amount is tax deductible. By reinvesting her tax refund each year she will actually be saving $1800. The remaining $500 a month will go towards savings. Carol has a number of options. She could:
1. Save this money in a bank account or similar investment and lose half the interest in tax.
2. Negative gear a property trust, after first having to save a deposit of 20 per cent. Taken over five years this would probably grow to around $38 000 and some tax would be payable.
3. Put her money into insurance bonds, or a spread of investments. This would probably give her around $39 000 in five years. A reduced rate of tax would be payable if withdrawn at this time.

Although savings are high, this is still not enough to buy property of the type she wants. The solution that I would recommend is number three, which provides a great deal of flexibility. She may get a much higher return than I've estimated. The point is, if she doesn't start, she will achieve nothing.

I've advised many people like Carol, some of whom do nothing. They look at the situation as it is now and decide it's hopeless. Without a plan they spend every cent they earn and have nothing in five years. Start where you are now and work on upgrading your expectancy. If you think small you will get small results.

Start saving toward a specific goal and you will usually achieve it in a much shorter period of time than you envisaged. Once you take definite steps, doors will open to you.

Plan for what you want by window shopping or buying small items that you can afford. It's all part of building a positive expectancy. I wanted a home of my own for many years, but it seemed impossible. Then I started buying towels and small items and putting them away in anticipation. An opportunity arose within months of my doing so.

Young marrieds—without children

Anne and Graham are in their late twenties and paying off their home. They both work and have a high disposable income which they intend using to build wealth, to enable them to have more options in future years.

They can save $150 a week. The amount goes into their bank account until they accumulate $1000, then they invest in various managed funds and insurance bonds. As they are still young, they intend speculating with a proportion of their capital, once they have established a safe base of $10 000. In five years time Anne hopes to have children and take five years off work. Both Anne and Graham contribute to a superannuation fund.

Saving $150 a week for five years adds up to $39 000. By investing in a spread of funds whose average return is 13 per cent they will accumulate $51 800. I have purposely ignored tax as they intend investing for capital growth, so it will not apply until investments are cashed in. As Anne is planning to cease work in five years, it would be best to place investments in her name. This way their portfolio could be structured so that they pay no tax at all as long as the investments were cashed in after her retirement.

Not everyone has large amounts to set aside, but aim for that first $10 000. This is the hardest step and after that your money will work for you. It is worthwhile setting this target as soon as possible. If $10 000 is invested at 12 per cent at age thirty, it could grow to $299 600 by age sixty. Wait one more year and you may only accumulate $267 400—a loss of $32 000 for waiting one year and it gets worse with each subsequent year.

Anne and Graham are only planning five years ahead at this time, but let us anticipate what could happen. When Anne retires she will receive around $10 000 superannuation, which she can roll over into an approved fund and therefore defer tax on this amount until it is withdrawn. To supplement their income when they have one less wage, they can convert their investments to produce income amounting to another $5500 a year. If placed in Anne's name this money could also be tax-free.

Five years later, Anne returns to the workforce and investments are again switched back for capital growth. This can be done by investing in unit trusts that allow you to switch from one fund to another. For example, they may invest in a property trust now, which pays income, but switch to growth units, on which they get the capital gain on the property later on. This eliminates paying up-front fees again. No more savings are added, as they prefer to spend this money to enhance their lifestyle. Only Graham continues to pay into superannuation. Anne may later on, but she still has her rollover money working for her. Their focus is now on having sufficient capital built up to ensure a comfortable retirement. At this stage Anne's rollover fund could be worth $17 000 and their investments are still worth $51 800, because Anne has been living on the interest.

By age sixty Anne's rollover fund could have grown to	$205 000
Graham's superannuation is estimated to be	$600 000
Investment capital could have grown to	$626,000
Giving them a total at retirement of	$1 431 000

For simplicity I've estimated average earnings on all investments to be 12 per cent.

Allowing for inflation to average 5 per cent per annum, their investments would have a value of $486 000 in today's terms. However a few per cent difference in the earning rate of investments could double this amount.

Anne and Graham will own their own home and have had sufficient money to provide a comfortable lifestyle along the way. Apart from superannuation, the only time they committed to long-term goals was the five years prior to having children.

No-one can predict the future, and all estimates are only based on what has happened before. But statistics prove that only a very small percentage of the population has planned ahead. The majority is dependent on government handouts in old age. With the working population dwindling and the numbers of aged increasing, this option will not be available in the future, so we have to provide for ourselves.

Married couples with children

One of the most important items for people with children is life insurance. If married, both partners should consider it. Term insurance is the most economical form. It works like car insurance, where you pay an annual premium for a certain amount of cover. Insurance is paid in the event of your death only, and there is no saving involved.

The amount of cover required depends very much upon your financial position. It should be enough to cover mortgage, all loans, and leave enough over to provide additional income to supplement lost income. Child minders and housekeepers all cost money, and the cost of being a single parent is often more, not less. Such insurance saves a lot of worry for the surviving partner.

Term insurance can be tax deductible in certain cases: if it's added to personal superannuation; if it is added to income insurance. The cost varies between insurance companies so obtain a few quotes or see an insurance broker.

Income insurance pays a regular income if you are unable to work through sickness or accident. If you are totally dependent upon your wage, it may be worth considering, but it is expensive. It is tax deductible, so this reduces the cost, but you have to wait until the end of the tax year to get anything back. Rates vary from one company to another and the premium can double. Most women pay a much higher rate for this type of insurance but a few companies do not penalise women. Low premiums are important, but ensure that you have the benefits that you want as well. Read the fine print; it can save you heaps later on.

It is sometimes difficult for families with children to save. Children have a way of taking all your money no matter what age—or maybe that's just my belief. Saving your family allowance as outlined under 'Sole Parent' is ideal. You may also wish to plan for children's education expenses. It can cost anything from $50 000 onwards to educate one child all through private school.

Education plans are often promoted by insurance companies, but beware of the charges. Sales commissions are built into these charges, and salespeople don't work for nothing.

If you have a lump sum available, then your best choice would be to place this money into a insurance bond and withdraw each time fees fall due. As insurance bonds have an entry fee of around 5 per cent, it is best not to withdraw from them for at least two years. If you prefer to save on a regular basis, choose a savings plan with similar fees to that of the bond.

Superannuation is also essential. Although there have been many changes in recent times, it is still an attractive investment. You must be employed, and work more than ten hours a week to contribute to a fund. If both husband and wife work, then consider both contributing.

Employers often offer superannuation, but you can also take out your own personal scheme. They are usually offered by insurance companies and some banks. Always check the charges and, if you can, contribute a lump sum to a superannuation bond each year, in preference to paying into a superannuation fund. The entry charges are lower and you have greater flexibility. This form of saving is money for retirement, so don't gamble with it—a capital guaranteed fund is the most secure.

Not all families are fortunate enough to own their own home, and for some people it is a dream that is getting harder and harder to achieve. Don't despair, keep on visualising and affirming, and be open to unexpected opportunities.

Sole parent families

There are two categories of sole parent families: those who get support from their former partner and those who are dependent on their own resources.

Saving on a limited income is nearly impossible, so it's best for anyone in this position to view their situation as being short-term. If you adopt the belief that this is the way it has to be forever, you will only develop a poverty consciousness. Remember, it is the belief that holds you there, not the conditions.

Looking back on that period in my life it is amazing how quickly time passed. Even though there was very little money, I never acted poor. My girlfriend, who was also in the same position and I went away for weekends at least once a month, kids and all, and we went out together every Sunday. There are many activities that cost little or no money. Even weekends away, spent in caravan parks, with the costs split, are inexpensive. So whatever you do, don't play the victim. You can still have fun on a small income and it allows you to expand your imagination.

If you can manage it, save your family allowance. Saving $52 a month and investing it at 12 per cent for sixteen years can accumulate $26 000. If you are good at saving, you can place this money in a bank account until $1000 lots accumulate. Then invest in a spread of investments such as insurance bonds, property trusts, share trusts, and term deposits. If you have a tendency to dip into savings, commit your funds to an insurance bond savings plan with low charges. Five per cent of each contribution is considered a low charge. Be wary of any plan that takes the first one or two years savings as fees.

Plan for the future by researching your goals, window shop for the things that you want until such time as your situation improves, and if you use visualisation and affirmations, it will.

Blended families

As divorce becomes more prevalent in our society blended families are increasing, and their problems are unique. Having two families to support is a wealth hazard, and it is difficult to keep your focus on what you want, if there is animosity between any of the parties.

There are a few options available, but choices depend very much upon the financial position of the parting couple and their feelings towards each other.

Property settlements are usually split percentage wise. Sometimes it's split 50–50, sometimes 60–40 in the wife's favour if she has care of the children. There are many variables, depending upon the term of the marriage and so on. If relations are strained and finances permit, it is a good idea to ask for a lump sum payment rather than on-going child support payments.

This lump sum can be used to purchase an annuity or be invested in insurance bonds. In either case, it can be structured so that you receive a regular amount, indexed to keep up with inflation for a certain term, at which time the capital will have run out. For instance $10 000 will last for approximately seven and a half years, if monthly withdrawals of $200 are taken. Allowance has been built into this example for this $200 to be increased each year by 6 per cent to offset inflation.

I particularly like this method even if the relationship is amicable, as it allows both parties to get on with their lives. Neither party is penalised for marrying again and it alleviates the pressure on the man to support two families. In some cases men use money to control women, and this option eliminates that factor and allows true independence.

Another dilemma can be the sale of the ex-marital home. If neither party has sufficient capital to repurchase, both end up renting and can get caught in a cycle that is difficult to get out of. My clients Jackie and Colin decided on the following plan.

Both sought advice before splitting up, unusual, but an excellent idea. Their family home was valued at $150 000 and they still owed $30 000 on a mortgage. If they sold the property they would both get $57 000, after costs, which is not enough for Jackie to purchase another home. As Jackie was to have custody of the children, Colin was concerned that they have a sound base, and not be upset any more than necessary by moving house. If they did not sell the property, Colin wouldn't have enough for another property either, and he was planning to marry someone else.

They agreed to retain the property in joint names. Colin would negative gear his half and Jackie would pay him rent for her half. In eight years, when the children were grown, the situation would be reviewed. Colin took over the existing mortgage repayments of $350 a month, and agreed to pay half rates and maintenance costs. This cost him around $5000 a year. He received $4200 a year in rent. This he was able to deduct from his annual salary, so the real cost to him was only $400 a year. Colin also planned to use his equity in this property to refinance a new home for himself. His much higher salary made this possible.

This is really the best option for Jackie as well, as she does not have the borrowing capacity to pay out Colin's $57 000. Meanwhile she has eight years to plan towards a new home purchase, and an asset that is growing in value.

Ageing parents

Often older people invest their money in the same types of accounts that they have always used, often to their detriment. If there is not a lot of money involved, I believe it is better to leave as is, rather than make them feel nervous taking on investments they don't understand. If large sums are involved, then go with them to seek financial advice.

I have had many younger clients bring their parents along. One client mentioned that her mother had a little bit of money she needed advice on. She was a sweet old lady, well into her eighties and I presumed she was getting the pension. Fortunately I didn't say anything, because the 'little bit of money' turned out to be $600 000.

With careful planning in very secure investments, I was able to reduce this client's tax bill by $30 000 a year. A copy of the investment plan was sent to her accountant for his approval and I made a tape of our meeting so that she could replay it later, as she had a poor memory. That was three years ago and the plan has needed very little review. Everyone is far happier, especially the accountant who had been telling her for years to do something to reduce tax.

Often we don't discuss such delicate subjects because we don't want to pry and parents may not necessarily want details of the financial situation known by family members. Specific details and actual dollars involved aside, what you do need to know is where your parents' important records are kept.

One way to broach this subject with your parents is to show them a list of financial records which you have made for yourself, and suggest they do the same. The list could show details of the Will and Executor, bank accounts, investment certificates, loan records, insurance policies and names of financial advisers.

Wills: Everyone over the age of eighteen should have a Will, and if your parents do not have one, encourage them to see a solicitor and have one made out. A Will is not a negative document. It is a chance to have your last say.

If a Will is not made before a person dies, (known

as dying intestate) the estate will be divided up as set down by law and this may not be in the manner wished for. The laws vary from State to State but in New South Wales the family home and a portion of the assets would be left to the surviving spouse and the balance distributed amongst the children. In some cases this could cause hardship for the surviving partner.

If infant children are involved, special provisions must be made to protect their interests. It is usual, where there is no Will for the surviving parent and children to appoint an administrator who could be a family member; however, the majority of family members must agree to this appointment, otherwise a trustee company would be appointed by the State. In all, the administration of an intestate estate can be a costly and lengthy process.

As well as making out this essential document, it is important to update it, as circumstances change. *Marriage invalidates a Will, whilst divorce does not.* It is therefore especially important that your parents' wishes are understood if they are divorced. If one parent dies, a new Will should be made and any investments, or the family home owned jointly by your parents, should be transferred into the surviving spouse's name. This will avoid considerable delays for the children later on.

An executor is the administrator of the Will and parents often appoint one or more of their children to administer the estate. Although this sounds complicated, it's usually a matter of consulting a solicitor, who will handle all procedures. If your parents left part of all of their estate to you, you would then become the beneficiary and you can be both the executor and the beneficiary.

Power of Attorney: As our parents age it may not be always be possible for them to look after their own affairs and in this situation they may give a Power of Attorney to another party.

A Power of Attorney is a legal document, made out

by a solicitor, which gives another person the right to act on an individual's behalf. The exact rights that are assigned can vary with the individual and they cease upon the donor's death or at an appointed time. Some cases when this could be used would be if your parents wished to travel extensively for a period of time and appointed someone to act on their behalf; or a widow, whose husband has always looked after the money matters, may prefer one of the children to continue the role.

Typically, a Power of Attorney can give the right to sign cheques and operate accounts, buy and sell investments, property, sign legal documents and submit tax returns. If a parent is sick or away from home, another party holding the Power of Attorney saves time, hassle and considerable expense.

Funerals are one of those things we don't usually talk about, but a time of grief is not the best time to make decisions which can involve thousands of dollars. An expensive funeral may make you feel better temporarily, but when the bill comes and payment is expected within seven days, you may be in for a nasty shock if you are planning for the money to come from the estate. Another consideration is the type of funeral required, whether it should be a cremation, a burial, or the family plot. Many parents make their own provision and you need to know what arrangements they have made.

It's much easier and more efficient to prepare and talk now before any need arises.

Widows

Three years ago Betty was feeling on top of the world. Her husband Paul had left for his regular game of golf and Betty was planning their first long-awaited overseas trip. Paul's retirement and sixtieth birthday were to coincide in two week's time. At 2.30 that afternoon, Paul suffered a massive heart attack. He died before Betty arrived at the hospital.

'It was totally unexpected,' Betty said. 'It never occurred to either of us to plan how I would carry on alone.'

In the following weeks, Betty was supported by family and friends, but as the weeks rolled on she found herself alone for the first time in her life and faced with decisions about her future. Like many women of her age, Betty had lived with her parents until she married. She had only worked for a few years prior to her marriage. Once married, Betty attended to the house and children, whilst Paul managed the money and made the financial decisions. Although the house and bank accounts were in joint names, Betty had always signed any papers when asked and had never taken much interest in financial matters.

'Growing up during the Depression made Paul very cautious; he was always a good provider,' Betty explained. The mortgage had been paid out a few years ago, and Paul's superannuation and life insurance amounted to a large sum. However, now that a regular salary was no longer coming in, Betty knew she had to make some financial decisions quickly. 'People assume that because you have money everything is okay. What they don't realise is, it's nearly as stressful deciding what to do with it, as not having any.'

Well-meaning friends and relatives offered advice and told stories of people losing all their savings. This scared Betty thoroughly.

Around that time she started receiving phone calls from a unit trust salesman. Although pleasant, he applied a lot of pressure. Betty almost agreed to his suggestion to invest the majority of her money in a property trust and live off the pension. 'He made it sound so easy and I didn't want to make any decisions myself.' Before signing, Betty decided to work out a rough budget, and realised that she would have to cut back dramatically to live on the pension. As she had a substantial sum to invest, this didn't seem to make much sense. Betty sought advice from her local bank manager.

Following her bank manager's advice, Betty invested all her funds in a twelve-month term deposit with the bank, at an interest rate of 12 per cent. 'That was lesson number one. Over the following months I saw interest rates rise to 18 per cent. I could do nothing; all my money was tied up.'

'The problem is it's such a vulnerable time. Just talking to the bank manager I'd break down and cry. I realise now it was not the time to be making major decisions. If I had to do it again I'd place the money in a cash management trust and make no decisions for six to twelve months. That way I could have drawn on my money at any time and the interest rate would have increased when rates went up.'

Another cause for concern for Betty were the letters from the insurance company addressed to 'Mr. Paul . . .'. As they were paying out on Paul's life insurance, the company was well aware of the situation. 'Yet no matter how often I rang and wrote to them, the letters continued to be addressed this way. This hurt me more than anything— it was a constant reminder.'

When the term deposit matured, Betty returned to the bank, but this time she took along a well-respected family friend. They were referred to the bank's retirement adviser in the city. His advice was to place Betty's money in bank-owned investments. Her friend advised against investing in only one institution. During the past year Betty had been reading the financial sections of the newspaper and had made her first visit to an accountant. As she talked to more people and her knowledge grew, she felt more confident about approaching an investment adviser.

She selected one from an advertisement in the local paper. 'Their advice was good, they wrote everything down, so I had time to read it all at home and they didn't rush me into a decision.' They recommended a number of different types of investments—debentures, Aussie Bonds, property trusts, shares—she invested with them and most of these investments did well.

'Whilst I can't criticise the firm I dealt with or their advice, I didn't feel comfortable with the man I saw. He was cold and made me feel inadequate. In fact it was a problem I encountered a number of times. People patronised me. Because I lacked knowledge didn't mean I was stupid.'

During the next two years Betty learnt as much as she could about investments, mainly by reading newspapers and magazines. Interest rates were high and she soon found herself switching money from one investment to another, to get the best rates. 'It gave me a tremendous sense of satisfaction and for a while I fancied myself as an investment whiz, but the novelty soon wore off.' So she started spending.

'I knew I needed more advice, so this time I decided to see a woman who had advised a friend of mine. The moment I walked into the office, I knew here was someone I could talk to.'

'I still keep in touch with what's going on with investments but not to the extent I did previously. Now if I'm in doubt about spending too much of my capital I just ring up and say 'Can I afford to spend $?.' The decision is still mine and I'm in control, but it's nice to have someone I trust to check things with.'

'Looking back, I realise I should have taken more interest when Paul was alive. We should have sat down and planned what to do if something happened to either one of us. But then it's very easy to be wise in restrospect.'

The most important thing is not to rush into any decisions. Putting the money aside for twelve months or so may not be the best investment, but it allows you to make a firmer plan at a later date, when you are more adjusted. If you have no experience at seeking advice, see more than one person, and read everything carefully. Choose an adviser that you can be completely yourself with, and never worry about asking too many questions.

Credit card addicts/compulsive spenders

Credit card addiction is the disease of the eighties, but compulsive spending is nothing new. Barbara Hutton, the Woolworths heiress, spent the equivalent of a couple of hundred million, in today's terms, in a bid to find happiness. Compulsive spending is an emotional problem, not a financial one, and if this problem is serious, then counselling should be sought.

When Sara arrived home after a two week holiday on the Gold Coast with her two children, she was confronted by a stack of bills. The holiday they had just had, the children's Christmas presents, the new school uniforms, the clothes she was wearing, all had yet to be paid for. As she would not be receiving a pay cheque for another two weeks and was nearly out of cash, Sara was planning to charge the groceries, the petrol, the telephone bill and her parking fine as well.

Sara said 'As I looked at the growing stack of bills I felt sick, but what could I do? All my salary goes to pay the old debts and there is never any money left over to save or pay current bills with. It's a vicious circle that I'd been locked into for years'.

At thirty-six, Sara is a vibrant woman with a major problem—she is a credit card addict. 'It's not that I'm so extravagant but having no money gets me down, so I spend. Sometimes we'll just get in the car and go away for a weekend, or go out to a nice restaurant. Nearly everything can be charged and it's so painless, until the bill comes in.'

Sara's children Ariana and Jeremy are aged eleven and seven. Four years ago Sara and her husband separated and at first Sara lived off the pension plus $40 a week child support from her husband. 'It was very tough trying to live on such a small income; there were no luxuries. I didn't buy myself a thing for two years, our outings were visits to friends or picnics, and holidays were spent in a caravan or tent.'

When Jeremy started school, Sara returned to work as a secretary. 'I thought my troubles would be over once I was earning a decent salary again, but they're worse. At least I didn't have debts before; I sometimes feel as if I'm drowning in bills.'

To the average person the solution seems simple: stop spending. To countless people like Sara it's really not that easy, because they are reacting to a situation they don't want to be in. Whilst married Sara was accustomed to a comfortable lifestyle. She tried to maintain this as a single parent, but her salary was smaller and she had additional child-minding costs, combined with the normal rising costs associated with children. As well, Sara did not want to deprive her children of anything they would normally have had in a two parent family, so she overcompensated.

For two years Sara had been juggling accounts but she finally reached the point of no longer being able to meet the repayments she was committed to. In desperation she sought professional advice. 'I thought that if I went to see someone they would take over my problems and I wouldn't have to worry anymore, but it didn't quite work that way.'

It's natural to want to offload a heavy burden onto someone else, but in these circumstances, such a solution would only be temporary and the problem would usually recur within a very short time. To solve her problem Sara needed the support and guidance of someone else, but most of the solutions she found herself.

Like many people in debt, Sara did not know how much she owed, nor what her living costs were. She knew it would be bad news, so it seemed easier not to think about it. Unfortunately, this type of thinking only aggravated the problem. Sara's first priority was to list all outstanding debts and the rate of interest she was paying. Her next assignment was to itemise all basic living costs such as rent, car expenses, food and so on, and variable expenses like presents, holidays, clothes and hobbies could be added later.

The total owing on her credit cards amounted to $5000, her car loan balance was $7000 and she had another personal loan of $2000. Sara was paying $600 a month in loan repayments. This would make her more depressed so her normal pattern was to go out and charge another $300 or $400. 'It's silly really, I was rebelling against my situation, yet the only person I was hurting was myself.'

'For four pay periods, I kept a record of everything I spent and I met with my adviser once a fortnight to pay bills and formulate a plan for the next fortnight's spending. Previously I had just banked all my pay and would keep drawing money until there was no more. Now I'm more organised.'

'Each fortnight I sent my creditors something, sometimes only $5 and I wrote to each saying I would bring the account up to date shortly, otherwise I'd be back in touch. I had to write, I know ringing would be quicker, but I couldn't face it.'

Sara's next step was to apply to her local credit union for a loan to pay out the charge account, the personal loan and to give her something to set aside for emergencies. The repayments for this would be $200 a month, plus her car repayments, saving her $200 a month. But first she had to draw up a budget and repayment plan to demonstrate to the credit union that she would make the repayments.

'Making out a workable budget was probably the hardest thing, because I knew it had to be one I could live with. The children had to give up their skating lessons and I planned our menu a week ahead and cooked a few meals on Saturday. That eliminated a lot of takeaway food and saved us quite a lot of money. I gave myself a weekly allowance. It was only small at first, but it was mine, to spend however I liked, and I started saving $10 a week.'

'The loan came through and the first thing I did was cut up the credit cards. Some people can handle them, but I know I can't. They were only small steps at first but I felt as if I was making progress. Because I wanted to pay off the loans quickly I've taken some extra typing which I'm doing from home at night and half of this money goes off the loan and the other half into a savings account towards an overseas holiday. I'm setting goals now and my spending is under control, although I still avoid the shops when I'm feeling down.'

'I was angry at first. I wanted someone to take my problems away. My solution might not be right for everyone but it's the right way for me. Professional advice made it possible for me to make the changes and decisions. That makes me feel very good about myself.'

Possible solutions

* Contact creditors and tell them of your situation
* Send a repayment on a regular basis, no matter how small
* Renegotiate a loan, so that repayments are at a level you can repay
* Seek professional counselling
* Be kind to yourself and always allow some money just for you
* Save on a regular basis, no matter how little.

Your own business

Buying a business is often an emotional decision. The high incidence of small business failure supports this. There is nothing wrong with emotional decisions, provided that you know what you are getting yourself into. Most people overestimate the rewards, and underestimate the drawbacks.

The first time I took on business premises and staff for my secretarial service, I was excited. To me this meant freedom. There would be no-one to tell me what to do, and being my own boss meant I could be involved in my children's school activities. How wrong I was. I was only in business a few months and I felt like I was in jail.

Unlike a regular job I couldn't take sick days, time spent out of the office was money lost. In those days we needed every penny. Rather than giving me freedom, I found it more restrictive than a regular job and the office rent and wages still had to be paid, even if I was not. It wasn't long before I sold out, fortunately at a profit.

The girl who bought the business from me had illusions as well. She spent a large amount putting in new carpet and fittings. She would come in some days and tell the staff she did not feel like working, so it wasn't long before she lost money. Within eighteen month she was forced to sell, this time at a loss.

Before taking on any business, make sure that this is what you want to do. Buying a shop, or a sandwich bar, or any type of business just because you want to be self-employed is a recipe for disaster. A business is COMMITMENT, and you must enjoy what you are doing.

Make sure you have enough money to take you through the crucial early days. Trying to repay a loan and support yourself from day one, places an enormous strain on you, and you tend to lose your focus. Have a contingency plan.

Do your research. There are many government and private agencies that give advice on small business, often at no charge. They can tell you how to make a business plan, how to market, and whether there are any sources of cheap finance, or government grants.

Record keeping is essential. Being too busy to keep records is a major cause of business breakdown. If you work out your profit and loss each month, you can act quickly to rectify any downturn.

Can the business support you and staff as well? Family and friends don't mind helping out in the initial phases, but you cannot expect them to provide unpaid labour forever. Some businesses simply don't have the potential to support more than one person.

Do you have any experience at this type of business? Running a shop may seem easy, but there are always hidden traps.

What competition do you have, and how well are they doing?

Do you have a business and marketing plan? Clients rarely just walk in the door. Most businesses have to be promoted.

If going into business with a partner, have you completed the shared goals exercise? Are you both committed to the same purpose?

Have you thought about what you can give to your clients? This could be outstanding service, or a product they cannot get anywhere else.

When you do work that you love, and you've taken the time to plan, then success will gravitate to you.

Summary

It's easy to teach and to tell people what to do, but the reality of putting principles into action every single day is not so easy. The principles in this book are simple. Simple but not easy.

The key to success is finding what you want to do and making life a hobby. If you want to stay as you are, that's fine, but if you've read this far it's likely that you want more from life. Refuse to accept anything less than what you want. If you work on changing your mental attitudes, as well as putting your financial affairs in order, you cannot help but succeed. It doesn't matter where you are now, it is where you are going that counts. Some days you'll succeed, some days you'll fail, that's all part of living, but ultimately you will achieve your dream and live an abundant life.

Glossary of financial terms

ALL ORDINARIES INDEX: A share-market index that measures the performance of about 300 stocks listed on the stock exchange. Can be used as an overall guide to how the market is performing.

ANNUITIES: An individual makes a lump sum payment to a life office and in return receives a regular income. Part of this income is tax-free. Annuities can be term certain, meaning you will be paid for a set number of years, or for life, in which case you will be paid the annuity for the remainder of your life. There have been many changes to annuities in recent times and expert advice is essential.

AUSTRALIAN SAVINGS BOND: Issued by the Commonwealth Government. A loan made to the government at a fixed coupon, which can be re-sold or cashed in before maturity date. Guaranteed by the Commonwealth Treasury, bonds are one of the most secure investments available.

BANK BILLS: A short-term investment, maturing within six months. Only for large amounts—usually $100 000 plus. Considered to be very secure as it is guaranteed by a Bank. Usually bought at a discount. For example, if you purchased a 180 day bank bill for $100 000 paying interest at 14 per cent, you would pay around $93 000 and on maturity you would receive $100 000. Instead of being paid interest on maturity you pay the lesser (discounted) amount up front and receive the full amount back.

BEAR MARKET: A term used to describe a stock or other market where prices are falling.

BONUS ISSUE: The issue of bonus or free shares to existing shareholders.

BROKERAGE: Charges made by a broker in the stock or futures exchange for purchasing or selling shares/futures on your behalf.

BULL MARKET: A term used to describe a market where prices are rising. Commonly describes stock-market.

CAPITAL GAIN/GROWTH: Profit from the sale of an asset such as shares, property.

CASH MANAGEMENT TRUST: Allows investors to pool their money to invest in the short-term money market. Typically these include securities guaranteed by a government or bank, but not company debentures, shares or property. Trusts provide competitive rates of return and money back on twenty-four hours' notice.

COLLECTABLES: Could by anything from antiques, comics, coins, works of art, books and so on. Generally the value is dependent upon demand. Traditional collectors' items tend to grow in value; others have only passing value. If interested, join a local club or subscribe to a specialist magazine before buying.

COMMISSION: Can be paid by investment companies to advisers. You do not save money by dealing with an investment company directly.

CONVERTIBLE NOTES: Similar to a fixed interest security but can be converted to shares in the company, at certain times during the term. See stockbroker to purchase.

DEBENTURES: A loan made to a company for a fixed period. Loan is secured by a charge over the assets of the company.

DEPOSIT: Generally classed as unsecured, the security lies in the strength of the borrowing company. Usually available from finance companies and merchant banks, interest rates vary and terms range from twenty-four hour call to longer periods.

EQUITY TRUSTS: Allow unit-holders to invest in the stock-market through a pool of funds managed by specialist equity fund managers.

Local equity trusts have many alternative funds available such as dividend imputation trusts, resources trusts, gold trusts. Some offer a mix of Australian and overseas shares. Dividend imputation trusts can provide tax-free income.

Overseas equity trusts can invest in a broad range of shares to a broad range of markets spread over many countries. Unit prices will be influenced by currency movements as well as stock-market developments.

FUTURES: A legally binding contract to buy or sell a particular commodity at a given time in the future. Normally a deposit of the total order is placed when contract is taken out. Deposits are set by the ICCH, International Commodities Clearing House. This deposit is usually the biggest difference between the closing and opening prices in recent times. The balance is not payable until a certain date unless the price of the commodity contract falls and then you would be required to pay a margin call. Futures contracts could be for anything from copper or wheat to government bonds.

Futures funds enable an investor to participate in this market and minimise risk. Futures funds can be guaranteed money back after a set term, or be subject to fluctuation.

FRIENDLY SOCIETY BONDS: Friendly Societies offer growth-only investments similar to insurance bonds. Tax is paid by the Friendly Society on earnings and the balance accrues within the fund. A bonus is allocated to your account once a year. If you retain your investment for ten years, the full amount is returned without any further tax liabilities. If cashed in earlier, your earnings are taxed and you receive a tax credit. In some cases, depending upon your salary level, these earnings can be tax-free.

GOLD: You can invest in gold by purchasing gold bars and gold coins. You could also buy gold shares, but these are subject to stock-market fluctuation, or jewellery, which does not hold its value for investment purposes as well as bars or coins.

Gold bars (bullion) are purchased from bullion dealers, most of which are listed in the phone book. Always take delivery of the gold yourself. It is safer to obtain a safe deposit box from the bank and leave it there, rather than to leave it with the bullion dealer. Insure your investment, as banks do not accept liability, and if the bank is robbed, you could lose your investment. Only purchase bars that are 99.99 per cent pure; the dealer can advise you of this. Smaller amounts are easier to sell.

The same advice applies for silver.

Gold coins can be purchased from coin dealers. Popular coins are the South African Kruggerand, the British sovereign, the Australian nugget, and the Canadian maple leaf.

INSURANCE BONDS: Are investment-only life assurance policies provided by Life Assurance Companies. Capital guaranteed bonds provide safe and consistent returns. The guarantee provides that your initial investment plus earnings once declared will not decrease in value.

Market linked bonds have returns which are often higher, but less consistent. The value of this investment may fluctuate. Market linked bonds are available for a wide range of areas including property, local and overseas shares and fixed interest investments.

No tax is payable if bond is held for ten years. For shorter periods, there is a tax credit the same as for Friendly Society Bonds. Depending on your salary level, earnings can be tax-free.

LISTED: Usually refers to stocks listed with the stock exchange.

MANAGED FUNDS: Often refers to investments in insurance bonds or unit trusts. The investment manager invests funds in a range of different areas, e.g., property, shares, cash. The value is subject to fluctuation.

MARKET PRICE: The current price to buy or sell a security.

MORTGAGES: Usually require a lump sum, which is then lent to an individual secured by a first mortgage. Fixed term and interest rate apply. Usually available through solicitors.

MORTGAGE TRUSTS: Your money is pooled with that of other investors and the trust makes loans to individuals and companies. These loans are secured by a first mortgage over the property involved.

PROPERTY TRUSTS: Your money is pooled with that of other investors for the purchase of property. Usually a trust will specialise in a particular area such as residential property, commercial and industrial property, or tourist resorts. Some trusts allow investors to choose between taking a high income or capital growth. Income from these investments is usually higher than other fixed interest investments.

PROSPECTUS: Document issued by company setting out terms of the investment. Must be registered with the Department of Corporate Affairs and only has a life of six months.

PUBLIC SECURITIES TRUSTS: Unit trusts which invest solely in government securities such as Commonwealth

Treasury Bonds and Semi-Government Loans. The highly secure nature of investments make these trusts very safe. Because the trusts actively trade these securities the returns can be higher than by purchasing yourself and holding until maturity.

ROLLOVERS: Suitable for eligible termination payments when you leave your employment. Include superannuation lump sums, accrued sick leave and *ex gratia* payments, but do not include annual leave and long service leave.

Lump sum tax is deferred when money is rolled over. Funds are available for withdrawal at any time, but must be withdrawn by age sixty-five.

SHARES: An equity in, or part ownership of a company. Can also be called stocks. The terms stock-market and share-market are interchangeable. Shares must be purchased through a stockbroker and the value of these investments is subject to fluctuation. You need expert advice before investing.

SUPERANNUATION: Provides for retirement, and special tax rates apply to superannuation funds that are lower than personal tax rates. If you are not a member of an employer scheme, you can take out personal (sometimes called portable) superannuation, usually provided by insurance companies and some banks. You can claim a tax deduction for your own contributions and employer's contributions up to set limits.

A superannuation fund is a scheme where contributions are added on a regular basis, often monthly. Charges can range from 5 per cent of each contribution to the first two years savings.

A minimum of $1000 is required for a superannuation bond, and additions in multiples of $1000 can be added at any time or not at all. Charges are less than for regular premium funds. Usually offered by insurance companies.

TERM DEPOSITS: Are loans at fixed rates for a set period.

Usually available from banks, building societies and credit unions.

UNLISTED: Refers to investments that are not listed on the stock exchange, such as property trusts. Therefore their value is not subject to stock-market fluctuations.

UNIT TRUSTS: Pool investors money and employ a professional manager to invest in a specialised area. For instance, property trusts are unit trusts that invest in property. Equity trusts are unit trusts that invest in shares.

You normally buy into a unit trust at the going price, which is revalued weekly in the case of shares; less often for property trusts. Your profit is reflected in the gain of the unit price. They can also fall in value.

References

1. de Castella, Robert, *de Castella On Running*, Currey O'Neil Ross Pty. Ltd. Sth. Yarra, p.4.
2. Hay, Louise, *You Can Heal Your Life*, Specialist Publications, Sydney, p.150.
3. Jampolsky, Gerald, *Love is Letting Go of Fear*, Bantam, Sydney.
4. Waitley, Denis, *The Double Win*, Berkeley Books N.Y. p.66.
5. Keyes Jr, Ken, *The Hundredth Monkey*, Vision Books, Oregon, p.11–17.
6. Bertrand, John, *Born to Win*, Bantam Books, Sydney.
7. Shinn, Florence Scovel, *The Game of Life*, DeVorss California.
8. Bertrand, John, *Born to Win*, p.145–146.
9. Bertrand, John, *Born to Win*, p. 145.
10. Ponder, Catherine, *Dynamic Laws of Prosperity*, DeVorss & Co.
11. Bach, Richard, *Bridge Across Forever*, Pan Books (1984) p.51.

Recommended reading list

You Can Heal Your Life, Louise L. Hay, Specialist Publications, 1984.

Love is Letting Go of Fear, Gerald G. Jampolsky, M.D., Bantam, 1979.

Dynamic Laws of Prosperity, Catherine Ponder, DeVorss & Co., 1984.

The Game of Life, Florence Scovel Shinn, DeVorss & Co., 1925.

The Double Win, Denis Waitley, Berkeley Books N.Y., 1985.

Index